THE SIEGE OF KOHIMA
THE BATTLE FOR BURMA

Once Upon a Wartime XIII

by
Robert Street

First Published in Great Britain in 2003 by Barny Books
Text © Robert Street
All rights reserved
Design © TUCANN*design&print*

ISBN N° 1 903172 35 7

Published by Barny Books, Hough on the Hill, Grantham, Lincolnshire Tel: 01400 250246
Produced by: TUCANN*design&print*, 19 High Street, Heighington Lincoln LN4 1RG
Tel & Fax: 01522 790009
www.tucann.co.uk

FOREWORD

"AT KOHIMA IN APRIL 1944, THE JAPANESE INVASION OF INDIA WAS HALTED."

THESE WORDS ARE INSCRIBED ON THE 161st BRIGADE MEMORIAL AT KOHIMA. IT WAS A SMALL GARRISON TOWN IN NAGALAND ON THE INDO-BURMA BORDER. THE GARRISON OF KOHIMA WAS A SUPPLY DEPOT AND CONVALESCENT CAMP FOR SOLDIERS GOING TO AND COMING FROM BURMA. IT WAS SITUATED ON THE MAIN SUPPLY ROUTE BETWEEN IMPHAL AND DIMAPUR WHERE THE BRITISH SET UP THEIR COMMAND POSTS AND SUPPLY BASES. IF THE JAPANESE HAD TAKEN THESE TOWNS THEY WOULD HAVE OPENED A GATEWAY TO INDIA AND, ONCE THEY HAD POSSESSION OF THE AIRSTRIPS AND RAILHEADS, THEY WOULD HAVE BEEN ALMOST IMPOSSIBLE TO STOP. THE ATTACKS ON IMPHAL AND DIMAPUR WERE EXPECTED. THE ENEMY WOULD HAVE TO BRING ITS ARMY OVER THE INHOSPITABLE MOUNTAINOUS JUNGLE TERRAIN TO GET TO DIMAPUR THROUGH KOHIMA. THE MILITARY AUTHORITIES DID NOT THINK THIS POSSIBLE. DESPITE THE JUNGLE CONDITIONS AND DISEASE, THE JAPANESE DID BRING THEIR TROOPS THROUGH, SOME FIFTEEN THOUSAND OF THEM, TOGETHER WITH THEIR EQUIPMENT, LIVING OFF THE LAND AND CAPTURING PROVISIONS AS THEY WENT. THEY HEADED FOR DIMAPUR. BUT FIRST THEY HAD TO TAKE THE GARRISON TOWN OF KOHIMA. BECAUSE THE ATTACK WAS NOT EXPECTED NO ORGANISED BRITISH TROOPS WERE AT THE GARRISON. THE INDIAN ASSAM REGIMENT AND THE 3RD ASSAM RIFLES DEFENDED IT. AT THE END OF MARCH 1944 THE 4TH BATTALION OF THE QUEENS OWN ROYAL WEST KENT REGIMENT WERE DETACHED TO HELP. 446 OFFICERS AND MEN ARRIVED ON THE 5TH APRIL 1944 AND THE GARRISON OF KOHIMA WAS HELD UNDER SIEGE UNTIL RELIEF CAME ON THE 20TH APRIL 1944. NOT MANY OF THESE LEFT THE BATTLEFIELD UNAIDED. THIS BATTLE CHANGED THE COURSE OF THE WAR IN THE FAR EAST AND BECAME KNOWN AS THE BATTLE FOR BURMA. MY FATHER, RAYMOND STREET AND SOME OF THE SURVIVORS WERE KIND ENOUGH TO SHARE THEIR EXPERIENCES WITH ME. THIS IS THEIR STORY AND IS DEDICATED TO THOSE WHO DIDN'T RETURN:

Those who gave their lives during The Siege of Kohima
Capt. J Topham
Lieut. G Inglis

CSM W Haines, MM	Sgt H Chantler	Sgt A Crathern
Sgt T Boxwell	Sgt L Peacock	L/Sgt T Morley
Sgt W Millichap	Cpl E Hatton	Cpl A Judge
Cpl G Fidler	Cpl G Martin	Cpl L Rees
Cpl W Moxworthy	Cpl L Rose	L/C R Bowles
Cpl T Rees	Cpl A Want	L/C G Mann
L/C J Harman, VC	L/C W Hill	Pte A Hawker
L/C A Hankinson	L/C S King	Pte P Williams
L/C F Worth	Pte H Allchin	Pte G Baker
Pte F Bennett	Pte G Bloomfield	Pte J Brattman
Pte J Brasdtreet	Pte D Bunnell	Pte R Cook
Pte J Coleman	Pte H Collins	Pte L Collins
Pte S Calton	Pte H Crosbie	Pte K Davies
Pte W Davies	Pte L Fisher	Pte P Fall
Pte W Forsyth	Pte C Foord	Pte C Gray
Pte A Guilford	Pte I Gwilt	Pte F Gipps
Pte F Hall	Pte J Hazell	Pte J Haslam
Pte J Hesketh	Pte H Hopkins	Pte P Hughes
Pte A Judges	Pte G Jones	Pte C Keating
Pte E Mancey	Pte H Norton	Pte D Oliver
Pte A Paris	Pte S Roberts	Pte C Robertson
Pte C Sims	Pte J Sinclair	L/C C Trussler
Pte J Walsh	Pte R Walters	Pte E Wells
Pte S Weeks	Pte D Windle	Pte R Gartrell
Pte C Williams	Pte E Whittingham	Pte A Williams
Pte J Williams		

From 5th April to 20th April 1944

INTRODUCTION

Although this story is predominately about the actions of the 4th Battalion of the Queens Own Royal West Kent Regiment, it must be acknowledged that the presence of Indian troops, loyal to the Crown, played an extremely important part of the defence of the garrison at Kohima. At this time the countries of India, Pakistan and Bangladesh were not individually distinguished and all local troops were termed as Indians. They were trained in the same way as the British Army but generally commanded by British officers. The overall operational command of the Garrison at Kohima was under Colonel Hugh Richards including the 3rd Battalion of the Assam Rifles which was permanently based there under the command of Major 'Buster' Keene. There were only three hundred and fifty of them at Kohima at that time. They weren't trained or equipped for an intense battle, their weapons were only rifles and kukris. The 1st Battalion of the Assam Regiment reached Kohima in late February 1944 under the command of Colonel 'Bruno' Brown, arriving from a training camp after being reformed after massive losses to disease whilst patrolling the deadly Kabaw Valley, but facing their first actions on the way at Jessami and Kharasom. Other organised Indian troops were the 1/1st Punjabs under Lieut-Colonel Neil Brodie and the 4/7th Rajputs under Lieut-Colonel Jack Cargill. On the night of 6th April 1944 members of the 20th Mountain Battery, Indian Artillery under Major Yeo arrived with a platoon of Indian Sappers and Miners under Lieutenant John Wright and a platoon of the 75th Indian Field Ambulance. Apart from these the remainder of the fighting contingent were a mixed bag that became known as 'the odds and sods' and included a variety of trained and untrained men that were present in the garrison at the time, such as mule leaders, drivers and clerks from the Royal Indian Army Service Corps; B Company of the State Battalion; composite companies from the reinforcement camps or those that had been convalescing after injury or illness. The number of fighting men present in the garrison totalled no more than fifteen hundred at most. Those men that were unable or not trained to fight were known as the non-combatants and numbered another thousand or so.

The Indian troops fought alongside the British men with a loyalty second to none. Indeed many of them came from families that had served in the Indian Army for generations. To some soldiering was a tradition that was deeply ingrained in their family history. To fight for the British Raj was an honour for them. In some villages it earned a man considerable status. Without their support it is unlikely that the garrison would have been held.

The Siege of Kohima - The Battle for Burma

CHAPTER 1

I took the Monday off in March 1942 and went down to the recruiting office to join up but they said I was in a reserved occupation. Anybody could have done my job. I wanted to be in the army. It was in my blood. My Dad had been in the 4th Worcestershire Regiment and fought at Gallipoli. That was where he was shot through the throat. He'd never been able to do a full day's work after that. I'd been ill when I was young and my father had sat on my bed and told me what it had been like in the war. I told the recruiting officer this and he said that if I was prepared to join the Army for seven years with five years on reserve service they would take me. I thought quickly and replied, "Yes," and was sent through for a medical. My hearing was poor I couldn't hear anything. A friend told me the answers before I went in. I asked to join my father's old regiment, the 4th Worcesters. I was in. I told Jackie Waring I'd joined up and he did the same, joining the same regiment.

My parents went mad. Mom was in tears and Dad called me a fool. He knew what was in store.

We gave our notice in and left our jobs. We handed in our uniforms to the Homeguard Stores. My mother asked if she could see me off but I preferred to say my goodbyes at home. We went to Norton Barracks for our training. When we arrived at Worcester Station, we handed our tickets to the collector. He told us to move along, saying, "No return from where you're going lad." I was finally in the Army.

I returned home for Christmas and rejoined my unit in Purley to see the New Year in. A few days later we were packed on to a troop train for Liverpool. It was the 14th January 1943. We boarded an old liner called the Mooltan. We were allotted a small area each with hooks and beams to sling our hammocks at night. They were rolled up during the day giving us room to sit at a long wooden table for meals. The ship was packed with troops.

We moved out but didn't go very far. The Mooltan stopped in the middle of the Mersey. We could see the large buildings of Liverpool. One of the men was from Liverpool but could only do the same as us, stand and stare. That night we woke up to the noise of the ship's engines. We joined the rest of the convoy at Greenock. We were detailed to carry life jackets at all times. We used them for pillows at night. We were also given a canvas bag with a small tin containing an emergency ration of survival chocolate. This was tied to our packs by a short length of string but a lot of us had ours stolen by others that would sneak up and cut the string. We weren't worried. We were confident that the convoy would take care of any U boats.

Nearly everyone was seasick. The floor of our mess deck toilets was awash with a mixture of seawater and vomit. The smell was so bad that many of us went up to the deck to lean over the side to be sick. I was too ill to hang my hammock and lay under the table. As we neared Gibraltar the weather improved and we were ordered to wear our tropical kit. The convoy split with half going to the Mediterranean. We went south. As we reached the African coast we were treated to sights we would never have imagined. A river, muddy in colour, cut through the clear blue sea. Flying fish played in the ship's wake and dolphins swam and dived alongside us. At Freetown we weren't allowed off the ship because of the fear of disease. The locals, many no more than children, rowed out, their little boats laden with fruit, nuts and anything else they could sell. Some of the soldiers bought things, others just looked. We went on to Durban and had five days there. We set sail protected by a small escort of destroyers. A lady in white sang Rule Britannia as we left port. She sang it to all the convoys that sailed from there. I think it was to boost morale.

In February 1943 we arrived at Bombay. It smelt foul and the heat was almost unbearable. We had a few hours to look round before we boarded the train. I'd never seen anything like it. There were snake charmers, beggars, knife throwers, street magicians who crowded round us hoping to get a few coppers. It was difficult to take it all in. The pavements seemed to be stained with blood but we discovered that it was the residue of betel nuts which the Indians chewed and spat out. There was poverty and squalor everywhere. Street traders, pimps and all sorts pestered us. Although my father had described the country in such detail, nothing could have prepared me for the sights and sounds of India. It was a relief to leave Bombay and board the train to Allahabad Barracks.

The old steam train on which we were to travel, was not the Pullman English style we expected but more like those used in the American wild west films with steps up to the back of the carriages and even an American style cow catcher on the front of the engine. The carriages were split into compartments to hold six men, three on each side. That was where we slept or sat during the journey. Some of the other carriages had open areas to eat meals or drink tea made by those on cookhouse duty. One of us would go up to the driver of the train when it stopped and get hot water from the train's boiler. We'd fill our bucket and add tea. Someone else would jab a couple of holes in a tin of carnation milk with his bayonet and throw in a handful of sugar, stirring it with the bayonet and the bucket of tea would be passed around. There were fruit and charwallahs at the stations. They sold fruit and tea in clay cups, working up to twenty-four hours a day for a pittance. The Anglo-Indians with us would call the fruitwallah and help us haggle and agree a price.

The stations were a fantastic sight, full of all sorts of people. The trains were never on time and people could be there for days. When one was due, the station guard would strike a piece of old railway track that was hanging by some rope tied to one of the wooden beams of the station building. Hordes of people would appear. It was like a scene from the Bible as they swept towards the train, dressed in their white flowing garments. All hell let loose when they tried to get on. We were all right. We were in the part of the train reserved for British troops. The locals would run up to the train and throw their luggage on, only to see it thrown off by somebody else. They all seemed to get on, hanging onto the sides, roof, or anywhere they could grab.

We stored our rifles under long wooden seats that lifted up. We would sit or sleep on top so no one could steal the guns. We had heard that Lee Enfield British rifles could be sold for up to a one hundred pounds on the northwest frontier. Not only were we sleeping or sitting on top of our weapons, all doors were guarded by armed soldiers twenty four hours a day and especially when the train stopped. As we travelled across the open country it appeared as if we were going back in time. The culture, the buildings were completely different to Birmingham. This feeling increased when we stopped at an isolated station and an armed Indian Police escort led out a line of chained Dacoits, wild looking men.

We eventually arrived at Allahabad Barracks, modern brick built blocks with the sports fields, plunge baths and all mod cons. Native servants, or dhobis as they were called, were provided to keep us clean and smart and would lay our uniforms on our beds and attend to all our laundry and domestic duties. A servant arrived at five o'clock in the morning and shaved us each in turn while we were still asleep under our mosquito nets in the long barrack room. We slept in a charpoy, an Indian style bedstead with rope weaving in place of springs and three coconut fibre cushions instead of a mattress. Four bamboo poles supported our mosquito nets. At the foot of the bed our kit boxes were padlocked and screwed to the floor. The rifle racks were in the centre of the room with the weapons secured with a long steel flat bar, chained and padlocked to prevent theft by locals. An indoor plunge/swimming pool was provided and a night time canteen. We had a compulsory bed down after dinner, sleeping between two and four everyday, the hottest hours, after which we would have tea at around five or six in the evening. Then we would have some compulsory sports and the remaining time was our own, unless we were detailed to guard or picket duties. At night, in spite of the fans, the air was hot, and the temperature still very high. You soaked the sheets with sweat and after getting up in the morning would leave a wet imprint of yourself on the bedding. It didn't matter though the dhobi would change it.

It all seemed ideal, safe, sound and healthy, but it was not. The weather got hotter and hotter and the monsoon rains beckoned. The heat was almost beyond belief. It was so intense that one man broke rank and walked in a tight circle and fell on the floor with heat stroke. As the months went by it got hotter and hotter. Many of the beds in our barrack room became empty and were put up against the wall; their occupiers in hospital with heat stroke or one of the other tropical diseases such as malaria or dysentery. This affected nearly twenty percent of the men.

The authorities decided that the battalion was to be given ten days in the cool clean air of a mountain hill station in the Himalayas called Raniket. Although we were to escape the diseases associated with the heat of Allahabad, most of us suffered some sort of climate change sickness due to coming from the hot sticky atmosphere of Allahabad to the cooler, thin air of the mountains. We were warned to stay in twos whilst walking along the mountain road, with its over hanging sides as men had been attacked by panthers and jackals. Guard duty was also done in twos without a gun, just pickaxe handles. The rifles were locked away.

On one occasion, I was woken for my stint on guard duty. I picked up my pickaxe handle. I was tired and half asleep. I saw a group of jackals rummaging around the dustbin area of the cookhouse but they immediately disappeared as if melting into the darkness. I wasn't sure whether or not they had been there at all. They had and they'd left for a reason. I saw a black head moving slowly from behind a grassy mound. It was a panther. That woke me up. I moved very quickly backwards, into the hut , shut the door and raised the alarm. Several soldiers then cornered the animal on the rocky slope up the ridge behind the huts. I joined them to see what was going on. The panther started to come up the slope towards us but soon changed his mind when showered with a hail of rocks and stones. It moved away quickly and, although I felt sorry for him, I reminded myself to keep my wits about me in the future. I could easily have been its next meal. These were not the only creatures to be wary of. Many a time, soldiers would be walking back to their huts with a plate full of food, only to have a hawk swoop down smash into the steel plate to steal the meat leaving the rest on the ground.

We did our jungle training in the hills of the Himalayas. It was torturous in the heat and thin air. My pack straps cut into my shoulders and its weight seemed to increase by the hour. In the oppressive heat of one late afternoon we marched along a mountain track, bordering a deep ravine with a rock-strewn river below. Apart from short ten minute breaks we had been marching for most of the day. We were expecting a surprise attack by a platoon of our own chaps. It was only training but they would be using live ammunition. They told us not to worry as they wouldn't be aiming at us. We weren't impressed. We started to move down, the trail widening, bringing us right down to the rocky ford of the river. On the other side there was a huge square rock, as big as a house and we made our way across the river towards it. When we were about half way across the ambush started. The 'enemy' opened up with Bren machine guns and rifles, churning up the water around us and whining around the rocks. Their officer fired his thirty eight-calibre pistol as we rushed for the cover of the far river bank. We fired back with our blank cartridges as we ran. Suddenly the distinct noise of a live round was heard coming from our ranks narrowly missing the officer. He wasn't pleased. He severely criticised our performance under the practice battle conditions but didn't pursue how the live round was fired. We never knew who it was or whether it was intentional.

When I told people at home about the training they were amazed. They said we should have fallen out. You couldn't. You wouldn't have a chance out there alone. It was freezing at night and a rifle that only fired blanks in an area full of tigers, panthers and all sorts of snakes wasn't any good. You couldn't see anything on the dangerous mountain tracks. A leg or arm could be easily broken if you fell. One chap did fall out and spent a night alone on a rock. They found him the next day. He was in a right state and had to go to hospital. He never came back. I didn't fall out. I kept going. I'd sing a song to myself, think of what I'd do when I got home or even about the hot meal in the cookhouse at the end of the day; anything to take my mind off the task in hand.

Jackie and I volunteered for a three day trek around Almora while we were at Raniket. My father had visited there many years earlier and often spoke about it. Everyone thought we were mad. They had done enough marching to last a lifetime and stayed in camp. About thirty of us followed our officer and an Indian guide into a hillside jungle trail, our packs stuffed with extra food. Their weight and the heat made us sweat. We lived rough and slept out on the slopes of the Himalayas, exploring the mountains and their streams, admiring beautiful scenery. Overlooking and following a mountain stream we saw a water buffalo standing in the water drinking. Large trout-like fish fed in the cloudy water about his feet. It was a wonderful sight watching him. The clear blue skies of the days brought bitter cold nights making sleeping difficult. We slept by levelling a space on the ground for our sleeping roll and positioned ourselves in the most comfortable position to keep warm, looking forward to a welcome hot cup of tea in the morning. I remember watching the wind forming snow clouds on the mountain peaks as I drifted to sleep. We arrived at Almora, but were not allowed into the town. As I looked from the mountainside it was just as I'd pictured it and wondered what had changed since my father was there all those years before. As we made our way back we noticed some small semi- circular, stone buildings called 'Dutch ovens'. My father spoke of these and of his unit marching through this area. They didn't have the luxury of lorries in those days and had to march and camp more often. Therefore, at particular points these Dutch ovens were built where a camp would be struck, allowing the cooks to prepare meals.

I was detailed to go to the Garrison Police Force at Lucknow with a small cockney chap. Our job was to police the area with the back street brothels, arresting anyone going out of bounds, improperly dressed or causing trouble. We didn't want to be in the police and were both too small to deal with any trouble. The Ghurkha officer in charge was not impressed. He took us into a nightclub and told us to go in at ten o'clock and arrest anyone who was drunk or causing a disturbance. Well, this was a drinking haunt of the Irish Fusiliers who were having a good time in the company of local girls. If they weren't drunk it was only a matter of time before they were. We decided we wouldn't hang around and made our way out just before ten. We'd only crossed the road when we heard screams, shouting and breaking glass. Our excuse the next day was that we were chasing some soldiers who were out of bounds but they had got away. The officer didn't believe us. He warned us that if we didn't charge someone soon we would be sent back. The next night we charged two soldiers for being out of bounds. They stood calmly with their hands behind their backs. When we'd finished they moved forward, showing their rank insignias on their forearms. They were Sergeant Majors and immediately told us we hadn't charged them properly, so they charged us. Fortunately our Commanding Officer (CO) traded our charges off against theirs but we lost our easy job as Garrison Police.

I met a beautiful Anglo Indian girl who was seeing her relatives off. It was eleven o'clock at night and we chatted. She was white with jet black hair and had a Welsh accent. She came from a rich family and was taking a Tonga, a small two-seater horse drawn cab, back to her hotel. I felt this was unsafe at midnight and obtained permission from the NCO to let her ride in our Army truck. I enjoyed being close to this beautiful girl as the bumps in the road shook us together and all too soon we halted outside her hotel. "Don't be too long Streety," said the NCO as I escorted her inside. A few minutes later a young black skinned man came to fetch her. She introduced him as her brother. I was shocked. I wasn't used to mixed families and found it hard to understand how she could be so white and him so dark. We chatted for a couple of minutes, said our goodnights and

I returned to the lorry and we headed back to our billet.

Our peacetime soldiering was now approaching an end and the monsoon was on its way. The heat was so intense that virtually all the vegetation had died, even the weeds. Everywhere was barren. A dead horse was found near the barracks. The poor thing had starved and vultures hovered around its corpse. They'd swoop down a short distance from the animal and then walk with their characteristic stoop, shoulders hunched up. They looked like little old men as they walked. On reaching the animal they would tear away at its flesh.

The monsoon broke and rain poured down at about two o'clock in the morning. We leapt out of our beds naked, dozens of us cheering and shouting. We stood outside letting the rain wash all over us, cooling down our bodies. Most of us had the red itchy prickly heat rash from sweating so much. Within days grass and plants grew from the hard ground. Leaves and blossom appeared on the trees - relief at last.

CHAPTER 2

It was October 1943 when we sent home our Christmas cards. They had to go then to be on time for Christmas. By then we were in the Arakan, a coastal area near the Bay of Bengal. I couldn't believe it, Christmas in the paddyfields. The Japanese had advanced, pushing our troops back towards the Bay of Bengal. After travelling to Calcutta we left by ship and sailed across the Bay of Bengal to the rice port of Coxes Bazaar. We disembarked and waited to board the trucks that would take us through the miles of paddyfields and scrubland. We were put on parade to be told where we were going. I was standing next to Jackie when the C.O. put his arm down between us saying those on my side would go with the Royal West Kents and those on Jackie's side were to go with the 'Worcesters.' So that was that, we were to be split up. I was now in the Queens Own 4th Battalion of the Royal West Kents, a regiment of the Fifth Indian Division (later the Fourteenth Army). It was December 1943 and the Royal West Kents had arrived from the Middle East.

The Arakan was a land of paddyfields with dense jungle covered foothills. It was to be our home for the next few months. Small or virtually dried up rivers called chaungs ran through this countryside, providing water for the paddyfields. Densely covered foothills stood out like small islands in a sea of rice. Each foothill was its own kingdom with the jungles and wildlife making a home for the animals. Across the Arakan lay our objective, the Tunnels. These went through a backbone of mountains called Mayu Range near the Indo-Burma border. These Tunnels were built for a future railway but never completed. If taken, we would link up with other British Divisions fighting on the other side but, before that, we had to push across the Arakan and clear the Japs from their foothill positions.

We waited to get on to the lorries to move forward. Dozens of native workers threw basins of water onto the hot dusty built-up road from shallow holes dug at the side, on the edge of the paddyfields. It was done to keep the dust from rising as the lorries passed. The dust could be seen by aircraft or Jap scouts. Despite their efforts the dust rose everywhere but fortunately no attack took place.

It was early December 1943, almost a year since we had set sail from Liverpool. My war had begun for real. The days passed quickly as our jungle training took place, marching through knee high grass without making any noise. We were told to watch out for leeches that attached themselves to the waving grass. One sergeant died when he fell asleep by a stream. He was covered in them and lost too much blood. We had to make sure anything that rattled was secured, especially during night marches. This was my first Christmas away from home and I can still remember eating Christmas dinner of roast duck and vegetables, washed down with a bottle of beer sitting on a bund wall to a paddyfield. We were lucky. The men at the front line had bully-beef and biscuits.

I had a feeling of wonder about this whole new world. I didn't think too much about the Japs. It never occurred to me that I might be killed. That always happened to the other guy. We were still very 'green.' We hadn't faced the enemy. One night as we moved towards a forward position and prepared to camp, the NCO told us to scrape an area of ground to prepare it for our groundsheets. I was getting ready when he noticed I had a white sheet in my pack. He told me to bury it. It was no use in the front line. We were ordered to take supplies of bully-beef to our Company, positioned on a nearby foothill. A sniper was shooting at anyone that tried to get through. Our officer had a brainwave. He suggested we pile several large tins of this bully-beef on a stretcher, cover it with a blanket and take it to the hill. He reckoned the sniper wouldn't shoot stretcher-bearers. We loaded up the stretcher and the officer told us to go. Part way across someone slipped and we dropped the cans of bully-beef into the flooded paddyfield. The officer shouted for us to pick up what we could and run back. Well I was in such a mess, I hadn't had time to do up my belt in the initial rush to leave and as I grabbed a tin my trousers started to come down. Nevertheless, I wasn't going to stand on ceremony. I rushed back as quick as possible, trousers at half-mast. We were lucky the sniper didn't fire. The officer then told us to run across with a tin each and we did but my heart was in my mouth the whole time. I think the sniper had gone but we weren't to know that.

The night was pitch black when we made our first infiltration through the Jap lines. We were to take over some foothills behind them. After several miles of marching we reached our foothill without trouble and dug in. By daylight a Jap sniper had found us. He fired from the hilltop at the heads of people. We dug a long crawl trail trench about two foot deep so that we were lower down with our heads below the bushes and out of sight of the sniper. We were learning quickly but they knew we were there. There wasn't any refund or second chances now. Don't think I was a hero because I wasn't and don't think I wasn't frightened because I was. I was scared but you had to keep it under control. It was a rotten feeling, creeping through the undergrowth knowing a Jap sniper could take a pot shot at you at any moment.

The next day the Bren gun carriers rolled up with our supplies and a party of men were picked to go down and unload it. A young chap near me was picked and he filed towards the Bren carriers and started to unload, directed by Company Sergeant Major Gammon. Five minutes later, a barrage of seventy-five millimetre Japanese shells blasted both the men and Bren carriers. Several people were killed including Sergeant Major Gammon, a shell landed by him ripping off his face. Another soldier gave a look of shock and horror as a piece of shrapnel smashed into his chest and he dropped dead. The Bren carriers moved out quickly. None were destroyed but the unloading party had been knocked about. We were shocked by the sudden barrage of shells. The young chap who had been with me survived with minor cuts and scratches to his ankle. He wasn't bothered and got one of the MOs to dress it and limped off to his trench. Later his leg became infected and he had to be taken back to hospital and out of the action. The Bren carriers came again the next day and this time I was detailed to the unloading party. I dreaded leaving my position to go. A barrage of shells came over but fortunately they were wide of the mark and no one was hurt. This time our own artillery replied and we heard shells burn and buzz through the air and land with the thuds of explosion on the Japanese positions. Our infiltrations continued and we eventually encircled the Japanese and captured the rice port of Maungdaw on the Naff River in early January 1944. They said it was an important port, but it looked like a couple of tin shacks and a jetty to me. We stayed there one night. We didn't get much sleep though. We were camped near some trees with a type of large grapefruit on them. They kept falling onto the ground during the night, with a loud thud and kept us awake.

Paddyfields were everywhere, but they were dry and empty at that time. Whether it was because of the fighting or that the rice didn't grow, I didn't know, but there wasn't any cover. You tried to avoid crossing them if you could but often didn't have the choice. You soon learnt the tell-tale signs like patches of earth pock marked by bullets. It was a relief to reach the other side of a paddyfield where the rice and scrub offered some protection. I preferred to travel along the chaungs. These were often lined with banana bushes and gave excellent cover. One day I was crossing a chaung and noticed I was walking in someone else's footprints and that someone was a Jap. They wore split-toed sandals so there was no mistaking those footsteps. They were only just filling with water and so he could only be a minute or two in front of me. His footsteps went one way so I went the other.

There were five companies: A, B, C, D and HQ. Battalion Headquarters (BHQ) was attached to HQ and the CO was there, so was the signals officer, the adjutant, the medical officer, signalmen and runners. I was C Company Runner, attached to Battalion Headquarters.

I preferred being a runner; I was happier on my own. I felt safer making my own decisions. I took messages and laid and repaired lines of communication, sometimes cutting those of the enemy. I carried a little book that the officers signed when I brought a message. There was no way of avoiding the issue. I'd never have got away with it.

We were detailed to roll out a telephone wire to a foothill in front of us. It was at the end of a banana grove that was growing out of the water at the edge of a jungle river bed that led to the foothill. The wire was to be laid through the leaves above, which grew in such a way that they formed a tunnel over our heads. Our group of men moved slowly, ankle deep in the water. We expected the sudden burst of machine fire or the crump of Jap grenades but it didn't come. We stood quietly in the water and darkness listening as the forward platoon of C Company moved onto the foothill without a shot fired. A few minutes later we advanced to take up our positions with the rest of them. After the signals had made contact with the new phone wire we'd laid, I returned to BHQ with one or two others to stand by for more running duties. The next few days would see me returning once or twice a day with messages to this position. In the days that followed Jap snipers moved in looking to pick off a runner and perhaps gain some information from messages carried.

I went out in the early hours of one morning with some medical orderlies (MOs). We were detailed to collect two bodies from the top of a deserted hill. These men had walked a few yards down a track and into the path of a sniper's fixed line machine gun on the hill opposite. Somebody had put towels over their faces to prevent the flies getting to them. I could see that one was a sandy haired NCO. I recognised him as one of the officers that helped to sort us out into companies when we first arrived with the Royal West Kents several weeks before. The other was an Indian soldier. Both looked as if they were asleep. They had been hit across the chest, by a line of bullets. We eventually got them to the bottom of the hill and they were buried as we stood guard, taking the map reference for the war commission to identify their graves should they want to recover the bodies. I didn't give them much chance of doing so in this inhospitable terrain. At least they were buried which was more than many of the others. As we waited for the men to finish we noticed another group of soldiers in the early morning mist on the paddyfields. Standing with our rifles ready to fire we recognised their jungle green uniforms. As they got closer we saw that they were one of our own guerrilla patrols. They had balaclava hats, faces blacked and most had Thompson machine guns without butts; geared up for close quarter work behind the Jap lines.

We'd been asked to volunteer as guerrillas soon after we landed in the Arakan but I didn't fancy it. I was glad I didn't when I found out what they had to do.

After a brief chat and a smoke, which was fortunately hidden by the mist, they went on their way and shortly after, with our job done, so did we.

I was then relieved from my duties. Someone took my place as BHQ Runner. I was detailed to a trench that was the target of a Japanese fixed machine gun. The first day I arrived, one of the chaps there told me what was happening and said that I could dig the trench a little deeper if I liked. When I got in I threw a few shovel fulls of earth out to tidy it up so to speak and settled down to my task. When the first sniping took place I thought I'd had it. The enemy machine gun relentlessly panned the parapet of my trench, the bullets zipping into the soil inches above me. I was sure they would come through the parapet and get me. I dug down a lot further. I dug to about four feet. When the NCO came round he wasn't too happy and ordered me to get an ammunition box or something to stand on because the trench was too deep, saying that we were here to fight the enemy not hide from them. I thought to myself, it was all right for him to say that, he wasn't in there when the bullets were flying. A crawl trench entered my trench. I was warned by some of the others not to look over in the daytime and only take a short look at night as the sniper would fire intermittently. They were right. Every now and then the sniper would let off a short burst of bullets in the hope of catching me off guard. It was a nerve racking time but I got used to it. I was able to move out via the crawl trench for meals and would nip into the next trench and spy through a hole in the forward wall to look for the sniper's position.

Whilst in my own trench, those in the neighbouring trenches would ask me to throw up an empty cigarette packet to see in they could spot the sniper. I did and each time drew a burst of machine gun fire from the Jap. I continually teased the machine gunner into wasting his ammunition by throwing a handful of earth or a piece of stick out of the trench. During the two week stint I was in that trench he must have wasted hundreds of rounds of ammunition.

Having to keep low down all day was boring and I would spend my time carving out holes in the trench walls to form little shelves and alcoves for personal things such as a tin of jam or bully beef. Food was in short supply and I had to ration myself to only a spoonful of jam a day to make it last. The rest of the time I would spend writing letters or reading. Now and then the guys in the next trench would invite me to look through their field glasses to see if I could see the sniper or any wildlife. I remember seeing a tiger eating a dead mule over in a distant paddyfield. I never did see the sniper.

Many a time the Signals Officer would shout for C Company runner and my heart would sink. One such time, I had just finished my breakfast of baked beans and tinned soya mince sausages, washed down with a mug of tea. Still tired from lack of sleep after weeks of two hours on and two hours off night guard duty, I hoped to rest a little after breakfast. Instead I was pushed out into the paddyfields and an uncertain future. I grabbed my rifle and bandolier of fifty rounds of ammunition and took the message from the officer. I started moving down the track off the hill to the paddyfields, passing bunkers and trenches on my way. Someone shouted' "Alright Streety". I gave a grin and a wink to hide the fear I felt and replied "Alright", and went towards the jungle cover. It was late January 1944 and, as I moved through the rice fields, I saw mudfish, only a few inches long, basking on the banks. They rushed back into the water as I approached. Flocks of green and grey parrots flew overhead. They landed on a dead tree, seemingly bringing it back to life with their colourful plumage. I continued to the distant foothill with my message.

A Jap patrol blundered onto a foothill held by the battalion and got wiped out. It was dark and they had been challenged by someone in the forward trench but instead of retreating, the Japs kept coming led by a huge Japanese NCO wielding a shovel, clearing a path up the jungle covered hillside as he went. Most of them were killed outright, but he kept coming in spite of heavy fire. Nothing seemed to stop him. Suddenly a grenade exploded on his chest taking part of his head off. Soon all was quiet again. I arrived on the hill the next day from BHQ. They had buried the Japanese dead but there was a smell of dried blood and death in the air. I delivered my message and stayed for a short while to look round. It was the first time I'd seen Japanese weapons.

One weapon, a type of Bren gun was much lighter than ours and fired a smaller bullet. Their rifles were longer with a French type bayonet, firing the same small bullets. They had oblong leather ammo pouches, grenades, helmets and water bottles. I noticed a type of short handled shovel or pointed spade for digging trenches and foxholes. I made a mental note to get hold of one of these shovels as soon as possible as they seemed better than ours. I did get one some weeks later only to lose it after a few days.

Shortly after, we infiltrated at night through Japanese lines and past enemy held positions. Lucky for us, the paddyfields were covered in mist and we passed through unseen, to take up positions behind the Japs, cutting their supply lines. The Japs soon found us and shelled and sniped our position killing and wounding a number of our men. They were not happy to find us behind them and even more so when our artillery, air strikes and dive bombers turned their positions from green to brown, blasting all the jungle cover away and causing landslides. Their foothill was lost to sight in the clouds of dust and smoke as barrage after barrage of shells smashed into their positions. Even so, after all this, they would open up with light machine gun fire to let us know they were still around. After one such attack, they retreated one night, using the mist just as we had done, leaving a few die-hard soldiers to slow us up. Soon after, our patrols reported - no Japs for ten miles - and we advanced to our next position.

We had to be alert at all times and took it in turns to sleep, two hours on, two hours off. It was a little easier to move at night but you had to let others know you were moving. We were all tense. They were a great bunch of chaps. We had a lot of cockneys with us and they were always joking. Two of them were great pals. One of them went off to the toilet one night and didn't tell his mate he was going. His friend later heard a movement behind him and fired – shot his pal. When he realised what he'd done, he flipped. He should have been sent back really but there was no way they could do that. He surrounded his trench with bushes so no one could get in or out and shot at anything that moved. I was told to tell him to stand to one day. I couldn't get through the bushes. I didn't try too hard. I feared he might open fire. I told the NCO and he decided to go himself. We all watched and waited as he went up the hill to what would happen. There was a lot of wild shooting, but after a while the NCO came back and Larry stayed hidden in his trench.

Being a runner I spent a lot of my time in no mans land or behind the enemy lines and had to learn very quickly about jungle warfare as the Japanese were more than experts in this field. I had to keep my wits about me all the time as the thick jungle vegetation of scrub bushes, trees and grasses, sometimes six foot high or more, not only provided good cover for myself, but also for the Japs. A sniper could burrow through a small entrance at the base of these high weeds and, once inside, an area could be hollowed out into a small room. He could then wait patiently to strike and even sleep in there.

It was around this time we heard that the Japs had surrounded the Seventh Indian Division in the pass on the other side of the Mayu Range of mountains to our rear. They had broken through and swept down the mountain road. The Japs had overrun a hospital, bayoneting wounded soldiers in their beds and chopping off the doctor's hands to prevent them treating anybody. Our troops were cut off but had formed a box like defence, where they fought off Japanese attacks and stayed put until the weaker enemy withdrew. Others cleared the area of enemy troops and repaired communications. We now had to withdraw from the hill we held and move to fresh company positions a few hundred yards away to the rear.

The new hill seemed nicer and more restful with no snipers. We were at platoon strength and I was still the platoon runner. My bunker overlooked the paddyfields guarding the track leading down to the platoon HQ and signals bunker. The platoon Sergeant was a regular soldier as were most of the old hands. They had been in action in the Middle East prior to being drafted to the Arakan and their experience was vital to us younger soldiers.

Our new position being further away from the Japanese gave us time to prepare our position. Around the hill was the debris of war, empty ammunition boxes, steel helmets, cardboard, cases and old newspapers. Some of it was from the British retreat of a year ago when the advance had failed and the monsoon had forced both sides into a stalemate in the flooded paddyfields. I decided to set up a dummy machine gun post using two wooden ammo boxes, some bushes with a dummy cardboard barrel thrusting out. Although a Heath Robinson technique, it would be effective to any advancing Japanese soldiers or at least make them think twice, giving me a chance to get a shot in first. I completed it by creating a dummy head of white paper finished with one of the old steel helmets. At night we would cover up surrounding tracks with bushes in order to confuse any Japs or at least hold them up for a short time. The next day the Company Commander inspected our position and praised us for our work.

Water was at a premium in our new position as there was no natural supply. One of the old hands soon showed us how to get some from the dry paddyfield. He dug a three foot by two foot deep round hole at the base of a hill. That afternoon the hole was empty but by the next morning it was nearly full of very clear water, gallons of it. It had filtered through during the night. Some of the men had dug up turtles while extending and preparing old bunkers and one old hand dumped them in the water hole to keep it clear of insects - basic but simple.

Many strange things happen during war. We were overlooking another foothill. We began to see cattle feeding on the dried out paddyfield and surrounding weeds. Young Asian village lads about ten or twelve years old were herding the cattle close by. While we were filling our water bottles they approached us, carrying bunches of bananas and 'jaggery,' a form of toffee wrapped in palm leaves and offered to sell us some. The bananas were wild ones with seeds in that could jar your teeth if you bit them too hard. We admired the bravery of these young village lads. This was the front line with both sides ready to fire at any time and all they could think of was selling their wares. They made several trips to our lines selling things. On one occasion they offered six-foot sheets of bamboo matting for sale. Some blokes bought them to sleep on during the two hour rest periods between guard duty.

This hill was alive with wildlife. There were all sorts of animals in there including wild jungle fowl. One of these birds really scared me one night. It strutted through the dark leaves and rubbish up the hill towards my bunker, sounding like a Jap creeping about. It was funny really, my eyes straining in the darkness to see who was there, my finger on the trigger waiting for the target but I couldn't see anything. I just heard these footsteps turning round a couple of yards or so away and going back down the hill, crumpling the leaves as they came back up. It was the next day when I saw the jungle fowl strutting up and down the hill in the same manner when I realised what it was that had cost me a night's sleep.

Another night I heard a rustle of movement in the bushes down in a hollow of trees. One chap was sleeping in a bunker above the hollow. I reported it to the sergeant, suggesting I should throw a grenade in case it was the enemy. He agreed. Unfortunately, the grenade hit a tree and dropped on to the roof of the bunker where the chap was sleeping and then rolled in front of it where it exploded with a loud bang. I'd started something. I heard our Sergeant talking on the phone and he said the C.O. wanted to know why a grenade was thrown and ordered us all to stand to and await the impending enemy attack. Most of the men were awake by now. I moved around to alert them. Two men challenged me to halt and give the password. I gave it and the other one said that I was lucky. His friend was going to shoot me but he recognised me just in time. I was not wearing my steel helmet in a rush to obey the order and had not heard their first low-key challenge. The Tommy gun that would have blasted me away was now pointing safely at the ground. I returned to my position and stood to for an hour. The order came to stand down as no attack took place. The next morning I got a load of stick from everybody. They had lost their sleep. I was still learning. Next time I would wait before wasting a grenade.

Later I explored the hollow from where I had heard the noises that night. Some thought it was a bear. They set a trap with bedding, rope and bully beef. The bear found the tin and the men pulled on the rope attempting to set the trap. Fortunately the ropes broke and the bear escaped. It was a good job really as no-one had given any thought about what they'd have done if it had been caught.

We moved on advancing across the Arakan. I was ordered to guide a party of men back from C Company to BHQ. The Officer gave me the route I had to follow. It seemed wrong to me. There was an easier more direct route by passing our old abandoned C Company position. In that climate, with heavy packs and full gear, the men would be very hot and tired having to cover that extra ground. But, being a good soldier, I stuck to my orders in spite of the barracking I got from those in the party that knew the route. After a hot and sweaty journey through the scrub and paddyfields we arrived and reported to the officer waiting for them. "Good. I see you didn't come through the mine field then," he said. The old route had been booby-trapped and no-one had told me.

Our next detail was to guard the guns that were blasting the Japanese positions on the Mayu Range. We moved behind Brigade H.Q. a group of us moving into something like the size of a football field with the jungle covered Mayu Range towering in the background. On both our right and left flank was a wall of thick thorn bushes about fifteen feet high and to our front a road. Flanking the thorn hedge between Brigade HQ and us was a small jungle gully blocked with large lumps of rock at each end. We were here for a day or two's rest with the somewhat easier task of guarding the guns from parties of Japs rather than front line fighting. The guns pounded relentlessly at the Japanese positions. We learnt that some seven thousand Japs infiltrated the Arakan, threatening to push the Fifth Indian Division back to the Bay of Bengal and promising a second Dunkirk. We pitched our two man tents in the open as we felt we were far enough behind the front line and there was no need to dig trenches for what would be only a night's stay. We wrote some letters and were able to scrounge extra food and beer and take things easier.

That evening we saw a lot of campfires up in the distant hillsides and a weaving line of flaming torches moving down towards us. We didn't take much notice and went back to our tents to sleep. We slept fully clothed, with our packs for pillows and our rifles, ammunition pouches and other weapons at our sides. We even took our boots off, we felt so safe. The bright moonlight and the knowledge of guards patrolling up and down our tent lines let us relax and I slipped into a deep sleep. I was dreaming of the noise of war when I suddenly woke to find the crack pop of Jap rifles and crump of grenades and light machine fire was for real. I quickly put my boots on, prepared my rifle, set my bayonet and got ready to stand to. There was no panic. We were hardened soldiers and instances like this were a matter of fact. The sergeant major gave the sentry a right dressing down for not alerting the men earlier and ordered us into the nearby chaung gully near the thorn hedge. A couple of Bren guns were set up at each end with an all round defence of the other weapons to try and secure the area. We were each given four grenades and crammed into the gully leaving our tents in the open ground. We were thankful for the thorn hedge as it appeared that the majority of the battle was taking place the other side of it, at Brigade HQ. No-one seemed to notice us, so we held our position.

Suddenly a soldier raced up from Brigade HQ shouting for the Infantry and was promptly arrested for leaving his post and put under escort within our gully to be returned to his unit and charged. We waited for the Japanese to attack our position, but the fighting petered out and we stayed in the gully until daybreak. The Japanese had retreated back up into the mountains. Later artillery spotters located them and started blasting their positions on the mountain side, the 5.5 inch guns giving them a heavy barrage of one hundred pound shells, turning their green positions to a dirty brown in a matter of minutes, with clouds of dust and landslides to deter them from attacking again, "No rest for the wicked," one bloke said as we set about packing up our tents and prepared to move to a more secure position. Unfortunately, the guns were only a few yards from our tents and fired a shell every half hour or so at night. We couldn't sleep at first but after a couple of days we got used to it and managed to sleep throughout the shelling.

My running dutijes continued. When I was taking one message, I took a track at the base of the hill and noticed an area of disturbed soil to a bank between two lush green areas. I approached it walking casually, but as I got to the pock marked bank, I sprinted through and kept running. The Jap machine gun fired just a second or so too late. This machine gun was fixed in position and sited to that small area of disturbed soil and was not able to follow me. I delivered my message to Major Shaw further up the foothill and returned down the forward slope at speed to the chaung and banana grove to safety, then back to BHQ for a meal and rest. I had to keep my wits about me all the time and made many more runs playing chicken with this sniper. He must have known it was me. He never got me.

The scrub lands bordering the paddyfields were covered with weeds waist high. The heavy dew would soak through my trousers. The sun beat down on my steel helmet and beads of sweat trickled down the sides of my face. The jungle green shirt I wore was wringing wet with sweat. The Lee Enfield rifle slung over my shoulder seemed to weigh a lot more than its ten pounds as I walked through towards the foothill where C Company had dug in. The Japs were on the opposite hill. Snipers were scattered around the paddyfields. I felt very much alone and scared as I got nearer. Suddenly everything went quiet. The birds stopped calling, a lizard with a call that sounded similar to a swear word was silent and all animals seemed to disappear. Then a screaming shell smashed into the paddyfields be-tween the two hills sending up a geezer of smoke and mud.

As luck would have it, C Company had a chaung with four foot high banks, with wild bananas growing in water leading right up the hill to where they were. After the shell dropped I took off for this cover and more shells crashed down around me. I leapt down the bank, ankle deep in water, but I was safe and headed towards our hill. Flying metal from the shells chopped through the banana leaves above my head, showering parts of trees and vegetation all around me. I waited in the chaung until things had quiet-ened down and worked my way up through a gap to the lower position where Colour Sergeant Jack Eves and the Company cooks were at the base of the hill in a high banked, tree covered gully, just off the chaung. They were old hands from the Middle East battlefields. They suggested I waited for a while until the shelling stopped and calmly played cards on a makeshift table. We sat there as pieces of metal ripped into the trunks of the trees and branches around us. I watched as a large piece of shrapnel came towards me. It was like slow motion. It made a strange buzzing noise and embedded itself into the tree inches above my head. I couldn't have got out of the way. Later as things calmed down, I raced up to Major Shaw's trench and finally delivered my message.

After handing over the message my habit was to go the quickest way down the forward slope at a run. You run sideways down a hill to keep your footing. I had done this for some days without trouble so off I went. Halfway down I heard a bang and a bullet kicked up dust on the slope about a foot away from my feet. I stumbled with shock but kept going. A crack pop of yet another Jap rifle followed me but, by then, I had the protection of the chaung. Vowing to change my habits next time. I raced back to BHQ a lot faster than I went out. A day or so later, I was relieved from my running duties and given a rest from that job. I was back with C Company on the hill. It didn't last long. Two weeks later the chap who took my place went missing. They decided to make me the runner again and this time, it was my full time job.

During the end of January and into February 1944, we moved onto a foothill to watch the attack to clear a main large Japanese defensive foothill nicknamed the Tortoise because of its shape. Many attempts had been made to capture it from the Japs. In the past days barrages of 5.5 inch shells and twenty-five pounders had changed the foothill colour from green to a barren brown and, at times, the entire area would disappear under clouds of dust.

Vengeance dive-bombers had been called in and a group of these flew up and over, appearing to have passed the foothill as they climbed high in the sky. They then circled and came down screaming straight at the foothill, releasing their bombs and pounding the enemy positions. Once more clouds of smoke and dust would hide the horror beneath. Liberator heavy bombers were also used to attack the Japanese, relentlessly pounding the enemy. As the dust and smoke settled, a burst of fire would be heard as the Japs let us know they were still in business.

At BHQ, we were asked to watch out for the aircraft recognition panels of cloth that our attacking soldiers would put out when they had captured the Tortoise. This was to stop further air strikes on our newly held positions. About an hour later we saw small figures in the distance, laying out the cloth and a huge cheer went up.

Although the dive bombers helped us, we had a lot of air support from two Spitfires. We nicknamed them the Maungdaw Twins. These two fighters flew over our positions every day supporting the ground troops. On one occasion we saw planes fluttering down like leaves. It was claimed they shot down fourteen Japanese fighters in a spectacular dogfight. Earlier in the campaign I saw two Spitfires flash overhead, heading home, pursued by Jap fighters recognisable by the large red suns on their silver wings and fuselage. We didn't get a chance to shoot at them. They were gone in seconds.

The Signals Officer called me and said that I was to take a message to C Company and pointed to one foothill very close to another in the distant paddyfield. They were almost identical. Not to lose my way I decided not to use the cover of the trees, bush and weeds that grew, in order that I could keep an eye on my destination. I would have to go in a straight line towards the hill and risk landing in enemy hands. Off I went straight across the dry paddyfields and hoped that no Jap snipers or patrols would spot me. I set off quickly and arrived safely at the base of the hill and stood and listened at the bottom of a small track leading up into the jungle scrub of the hillside. I heard people talking. I moved up the track thinking C Company had arrived. I bumped into four Indian soldiers in a weapon pit with a large radio set, all dressed in British jungle green uniforms. Straight away I took them for some artillery operational unit of our Brigade and asked them in English if the Royal West Kents were on the hill anywhere. They looked very worried and did not speak and just shook their heads and packed all their equipment away. I felt uneasy and decided not to hang around and retraced my steps back down the hill. I just reached the foot of the hill to meet Major Watts leading a group of C Company men in my direction. "I see you have got to the hill before us Private Street." he said, grinning at me along with all the others. This embarrassed me so much that I forgot to tell him about the group of Indians and their radio. Later, we heard units of the Indian National Army or JIFFS (Japanese Indian Fighting Force) as they were named, were operating against us in this area, fighting with the Japs. These Indians were probably JIFFS. Anyway I passed the message over to Major Watts and headed for BHQ wondering whether I'd had another near miss and thought myself lucky to be alive.

The Battalion moved up to a forward position and awaited darkness. When it arrived the mist fell. We advanced on to the paddyfields passing Japanese positions on the jungle covered foothills. During the first hour out a lone sniper opened up with a light machine gun, probably hearing us rather than seeing us. His tracer bullets floated high over the column and harmlessly into nowhere. There was no panic. We just kept marching at the same pace moving deeper into enemy territory, leaving the sniper behind, marking his position for others to deal with later. We pushed onto our objective and, at first light, we dug in to the paddyfields near a village by the Naff River. While there, Tom Hogg, a B Company officer used gun cotton with short fuses to do a spot of 'fishing.' We needed to improve our supplies and that was the quickest method.

We infiltrated twelve miles behind the Japanese lines. Some of the Indian troops were to take a village and we were in support. The Indian troops attacked the village just before first light with artillery support and air strikes. We consolidated our position and waited for further orders. The battle was raging with the crump of mortar bombs, grenades and the crack-pop of the Jap rifles all around. The heavy burst of the replying Bren guns could be distinctly heard. We could see some of the bashas on fire, others were smoking. Then, the Signals Officer called me and pointed to the burning village and told me find my Company position. I collected the written message and set off across the flat paddyfields towards the palms and other trees around the burning chaos in front of me. I hadn't much of a clue where to find them.

As I reached the village, things looked worse than I'd thought. I began meeting men, women and children, all panic stricken villagers, frightened pale under their tan, fleeing from the battle torn area. I could hear grenades going off and mortar bombs exploding, together with machine gun and small arms fire. I couldn't find C Company and headed for the road that went straight into the village centre. When I got there I spotted some Indian soldiers dashing around among the burning huts. One dashed out of the smoke and on to the road. The wild eyed Indian soldier with his fixed bayonet glared at me, but I calmly asked him if he had seen the West Kents around. He looked at me as if I was mad, shook his head as if he didn't understand and dashed back into the smoke. I continued along and out the other side of the village, onto a built up road passing through open paddyfields. There was a large iron bridge several hundreds yards in front of me. I spotted distant movement on the bridge. I hesitated and decided to check it out as I thought it may be C Company. If not, I would go back into the village. I slung my rifle and started for the bridge. The road was six feet higher than the paddyfields. Thick bush, rushes and weeds bor dered each side. This was the bridge over the Naff River. I could make out matchstick size figures in the distance. I realised that they had seen me and were taking up positions of defence. They were Japs and I'd come too far and ended up behind enemy lines. I slowly turned and walked off in a normal fashion, eventually making it to a safe distance, out of range of the enemy guns.

I approached the burning village for a second time and as I looked over-head I heard a roar of aircraft machine gun and cannon fire. I saw a Jap plane blasting the side out of one of our Spitfires. As the Jap aircraft peeled off, the Spitfire trailed black smoke eventually crashing near another village on some distant paddyfield. After further searching I eventually located my Company, well to the rear of the village and delivered the message. The fighting continued and the Japanese eventually retreated to the large iron bridge into which I had nearly blundered.

Fire was a continuous hazard in the long, hot, dry periods in this area of the Arakan. The place where we were had a small river flowing through the paddyfields, surrounded by an area of bushland and jungle covered foothill positions. A fire started on one occasion, probably caused by mortar fire. This drove a mixed bag of Indian, British and Japanese soldiers off their foothill positions. Our Company cooks on one foothill had just cooked dinner. The flames from the bush fire started burning trees and bushes around their position. They were ordered to leave for the nearby river and shelter until the fire had passed. They dropped the dixies or food contain-ers with the dinner in them down into deep slit trenches to prevent them from being burnt. When they returned they served a late dinner, still hot, kept warm by the fire. During this mayhem we all started to cut fire breaks sometimes having to dash and take cover in the river as sparks and embers settled on our packs. Luckily we were wearing steel helmets, but many were burnt and had to jump into the nearby water. The war stopped for a short while as friend and foe alike fought nature, rather than each other. Eventually wind and firebreaks were completed and the fire burnt itself out leaving smoke charred foothills, baring their black peaks. Our posi-tions and those of the enemy were refilled and business of war continued.

I returned to BHQ for more work and heard that the fire ridden village was eventually taken by our troops a day or two later. We heard that some more mail had arrived and I eagerly moved forward to collect my letters and a bundle of newspapers. In a quieter moment I started to read the newspapers in my trench but it was early evening and the Sergeant ordered us to stand to. He said, "Another day tomorrow Street, to read your papers. Get on with the job in hand." I put the papers down and leant forward in a position of readiness rifle and bayonet resting on the parapet of my trench. Another night of lack of sleep was to lie ahead, two hours on and two hours off guard throughout the night and for all the nights to come. I looked out on to the now darkening paddyfields with mixed feelings and a touch of homesickness.

As the darkness fell the noise of frogs and insects took over. My eyes strained into the darkness as I looked down the track for signs of any danger. This was our way of life now and for many months to come. As dawn approached, part of the night time sky lightened. This was a relief to us that were forcing ourselves to stay awake after days of lack of sleep and nights of guard duty almost taking us to breaking point with exhaustion. As the sun rose, the quiet order to stand to was given. Men still asleep were shaken awake to take up positions of defence all over the hill. It was a quiet morning. We were on the offensive with fixed positions for a few days. We were more relaxed as we were now chasing the Japs rather than them chasing us.

We moved to a small jungle covered foothill, almost as high as a tower block, standing in the paddyfields like some castle which, would be protected by its moat in the rainy season. It was covered in straw coloured rice waiting to be harvested. This foothill was typical of the many stretching away to the distance to meet with the Mayu Range of mountains that seemed to reach up to the sky. We checked our weapons and other routine things after standing down. These were all the things that were neglected when the enemy were chasing us. We had no time then.

Here at BHQ the Signal Platoon enjoyed a cowboy's breakfast of baked beans and tinned bacon, with hard biscuits and a cup of tea. As they ate some signallers were already working, raising the rifle companies and radioing through the orders for the day.

"I say again, Able, Baker, Charlie, Dog. Come in please." the noise continued to drone into the warm air as others rested, ate and dozed. The work of the day went on and a call was heard for one chap or another to attend to some routine duties but I continued to rest. It was short lived as I, C Company runner, was called over by the Signals Officer to take a message to the Company H.Q. I moved down the track to the paddyfields on to scrubland of the wet knee high weeds. I didn't relish another day of wet feet and for perhaps an hour or two an unknown future. I quickly went to a distant jungle clad foothill where C Company was dug in. But again I was lucky and once again I survived unscathed, the message safely delivered.

The weather was extreme. An early morning mist and heavy dew would leave the area soaking wet. The high humidity would drench my clothes and my feet would be wet through. Once the early morning mists lifted, the hot sun would soon dry us out. Then our uniforms became drenched with sweat. We had a tropical storm one night. We runners were busy putting up rough shelters over our rest area, using branches or whatever was available. Suddenly John Harman, from D Company, appeared with a patrol. He suggested I used banana leaves to make the roof more watertight. He was killed a few weeks later at Kohima.

Some time later, I followed a small high banked stream at the side of the paddyfields. I was taking my time, watching mud fish run down the muddy banks of the streams, dodging eel holes full of water which moved up and down showing that the eels were at home. The locals tied a maggot to a piece of string and left it over these holes, waiting for the eel to take the bait. They soon did and dragged the bait and line into their hole, only for it to be pulled out with the eel attached. It was like pulling a cork from a bottle. Later, when the war had ended, we tried this method. We gave those we caught to the young Burmese children watching us.

I entered a chaung leading to our foothill through a gap in the high bank used by Company cooks to get water for the evening hot meals and tea. Soon I left the ankle deep water and moved on to the semi-dry cover of the weed and scrub on the edge of sun dried, unworked paddyfields and quickly crossed an open area on the way to BHQ. Near the edge of the paddyfield, I stopped near a paddy bund. I saw a figure of a soldier coming towards me. I hid behind the paddy bund, readying my 303 rifle, focusing it on him. After a moment he came into full view, his English shaped steel helmet and his jungle green uniform giving him away. I recognised him as A Company Runner.

We met up and chatted for a few minutes and he suggested that we sat down and had a smoke instead of rushing back. It seemed a good idea. A Company Runner placed his netted steel helmet between his feet and rested his Thompson machine gun between his legs, holding the pistol grip with one hand and lighting our cigarettes with the other. Everything was quiet and peaceful, the call of doves, wood birds and insects could be heard, as we relaxed with our cigarettes. I had done my job, delivering my message and was on my way back to BHQ for a welcome rest. Suddenly, his gun went off, thankfully only a single shot instead of an automatic burst. He had inadvertently squeezed the trigger. It made a hell of a racket in the quiet jungle as the bullet shot into his helmet and rattled around until it came to a standstill. Neither of us were injured and the bullet eventually ended up as a flattened lump of metal trapped in the helmet netting. I called him for everything. We immediately took cover in the surrounding scrub and made our way back to BHQ.

We continued our push forward towards the Mayu Range, an unforgiving place, which was difficult to map properly. It was a maze of small peaks and thick jungle, with a network of dry chaungs. Off the road, most tracks were game tracks made by elephants, tigers, panthers and other animals. We could hear them at night.

The carnage of war was everywhere; dead bodies in differing stages of decomposition, some stripped to skeletons by the animals and insects of the jungle. Weapons and equipment lay strewn all over the place. I found a brand new Japanese helmet with cover and net when I was moving back down a chaung with a message. I looked at it for a few minutes trying to decide whether to keep it or not but souvenirs of any weight or size were an additional burden, so I left it.

The Japs had dug well into the ridges above the Tunnels. We infiltrated one night, moving through the paddyfields. We moved in the darkness in single file. Our mules were loaded with supplies, ammunition and equipment. We marched all night past foothills and through the dry paddyfields. It was now March 1944.

As dawn broke on the misty paddyfields, a mule let out a loud braying noise and the other mules joined in. At the same time, someone saw a Jap dashing away into the bush and scrub and into the jungle at the edge of the paddyfield we were crossing. We halted and started to organise defensive positions when the first Jap seventy five millimetre shell screamed over our heads, landing on the BHQ area behind us. About thirty shells fell mostly to our rear. We scraped out shallow trenches in the rock hard ground of the open area of the paddyfield, sweating in the heat of the morning sun. There was a rumble of guns as our artillery spotter eventually pin-pointed the Jap gun and our own shells came over our heads, with a loud burning, whispering sound. The loud bangs of their explosions some-where in the hills in front of us quietened down the Japanese artillery and no more shells were fired at us. We had suffered losses, including our Signals Officer's batman and this upset the officer a great deal. The chap who had replaced me as C Company runner was also injured. The next day B Company led the advance and asked for artillery support to soften up the enemy. Unfortunately it fell short. The guns fired at least two salvoes before they were silenced and that was by word of mouth. The radio was damaged by the first salvo. William Robinson was among the seventeen killed and a further forty one wounded.

C Company prepared to move further forward. I was Company Runner again, replacing the wounded chap. We moved to a ridge like foothill with BHQ Company. There were several old Jap foxholes, all in a line, dug about two foot lower than the track. When we struggled in through the small oval entrances, built into the cliff like sides of the ridge we found each foxhole had been enlarged to take three men, able to lie side by side. The roof was very close to our heads. It was very claustrophobic, so I made sure that I would be the last man in and near the opening, when we used them to sleep in at night whilst on guard. The next day we moved to another position and stayed there for a few days. I would take messages to and from the Company whilst they dug into their new positions. My runs went past the remains of the blown up metal bridge that spanned the River Naff.

As time went by I got more used to being a runner and more relaxed, even having the chance to pop in and look at an old Japanese deserted roadside cookhouse, later to be occupied by BHQ, on the side of the road leading to the Tunnels. I used to wander off the road and into the cookhouse and had a look for anything that might be of value or interest. I only found a pair of old wooden sandals that were of no real use and threw them away. When I turned round I was quite shocked to find I was looking into two foxholes, either side of the track that I had just come down. If they had been occupied I would have been shot in the back. I investigated the foxholes and found that they led out to either side of the road and back into the cookhouse. If you chased an enemy through one he could double back behind you.

I was still attached to the Signals Platoon of HQ Company, as runner for C Company. Shot at by snipers and near misses from shell fire, out on open paddyfields were all part of the job. This was my third time as runner. The others had been killed or wounded. One was found in a minefield next to the body of a dead Jap. Circling vultures drew the attention of the patrol looking for him. We moved towards thick jungle and mountain area near the Tunnels. I moved up with BHQ, taking up positions in the bamboo forest at the side of a chaung, digging in a few yards from a bend in the dry riverbed. To our left was the road leading to the Tunnels about two hundred yards away. These Tunnels were built for some forgotten railway to go beneath the mountains of the Mayu Range. Now the enemy occupied them and it was our job to get them out.

Behind the road were the rain forests and the jungles of the Mayu Range. Our rifle companies were digging in on ridges close to the Japanese positions. High above us were well defended Japanese ridges, overlooking the Tunnels. The road to the Tunnels had a dried up chaung to the right hand side with a bed of small rocks and gravel and a six foot high bank up to the road itself with jungle covered mountains beyond. To the other side of the chaung was a bank of large rocks, three or four feet high, forming pools that stank of the dead fish which had been trapped as the river had dried up. This bank continued into the bamboo jungle.

The Japs would have seen us if we had gone any further. They controlled that part of the chaung and covered it with machine guns from the ridges above the Tunnels. One of our leading patrols had run into some machine gun fire from those Jap positions. A dead British soldier lay in the chaung and stayed where he had fallen. A Jap machine gun covered his body, perhaps for days, waiting for some of his comrades to come and move him. We waited where we were on our side of the bend. There was no hurry in the dried up river bed and we were well hidden. I crossed the road and ran down with the messages as some men repaired field phone lines hit by mortar or shell fire. It was essential that any damaged lines were repaired immediately to maintain our lines of communication and we worked continuously to keep things operational.

As we dug in our slit trenches several shells whispered over our heads going towards the Japanese lines. A signaller hidden somewhere in the clump of bamboo trees started to operate his radio set. "Come in Able, Baker, Charlie, Dog." I listened to the signaller's voice drifting into the still air in the heat of the chaung. The crack pop sound of the Jap snipers rifle sent a bullet whining down the chaung and a Bren gun answered with a heavy short burst of the recognisable 'Johnny get you gun' sound. The mountains echoed with the thunder of the shells exploding on the Jap positions near us. The signaller from the bamboo clump tried again to contact our rifle companies and eventually got through. A distant clump of grenades and light automatic fire told me that things were hotting up. Then, someone called for C Company Runner. Now it was my turn to take the risks again in the rain forests. As I got up I heard the crack pop of a Jap sniper's rifle from the jungle covered mountainside.

The I (Intelligence) Section Officer was to show me how to get to the new C Company position and we raced across the chaung with me rushing to keep up with him. We climbed up the bank, across the road and dashed into the jungle on to an old track or game trail, following some lines of communication. We began to move up the mountainside among the trees and bushes, some with thorns that tore at our uniforms as we climbed higher. In parts the ground was soft with a mixture of rotten leaves and stinking mud. The stench was helped along with the sweltering heat and a Turkish bath kind of climate. We were both soaked to the skin with sweat as we climbed. After going up one hundred yards or so, the ground levelled out to a row of privet bushes overlooking the road. The Officer said, "Keep you head down here, we are in full view of the enemy. If you look through the hedge you can see the Tunnels with the Jap positions on top." We moved quickly past this hedge having a quick look as we passed. I nicknamed this hedge 'The Privet' and it served as a landmark for me in future runs. On this game trail was an area of trampled down trees, with football size balls of elephant dung and watery holes in the mud where their feet had sunk in. I nicknamed this area the' Assault Course' as we started to climb over the many tree trunks, some quite large. We continued to climb higher and then, to my relief, we started to go downhill and found ourselves back in another part of the chaung,, with C Company dug in on a ridge nearby. The Intelligence Officer decided to stay and turned to me and said,"Well off you go now Street." I took off straight away. This was no place to hang about and with a quick look at the Tunnels as I past the Privet, I soon arrived back at BHQ.

I was asked to take a small mixed party of men to C Company. Some would stay and three others from HQ were returning. I was to guide them out and get back as quickly as possible for more duties. For the next few days I would do that little trip daily, taking messages, guiding groups of men to and from my Company position, helping to repair the telephone wire damaged by shells. However the first one didn't go to plan. Off we went with all going well. I made the mistake of telling them how they could see the Tunnels from the privet bushes. I was shocked as they all took a good long look, acting like tourists on a visit to a historic place. I had to be firm and tell them that the Japs could see them and we should get on our way as quickly as possible. We came to the fork in the communication wire and for one moment I couldn't remember which direction to follow. The men started to barrack me, so I chose the left hand fork. I felt I had made a mistake but was too stubborn to admit it, yet I hoped the wire would lead to a chaung. We climbed up the mountainside. We were all soaking wet with sweat. Some men were swearing and cussing because of the arduous route. We eventually came to a twelve foot dry waterfall and I knew by then that this was not the right trail but I dare not tell them, not yet anyway. We climbed the waterfall and continued about fifty yards higher up towards the thicket of high thorn that blocked the track. The end of the telephone line lay nearby. It was a dummy line. They all looked at me with shocked expressions on their faces. We could hear voices behind the thicket and they were not speaking English. Some of my men were Eastenders and didn't suffer fools gladly but didn't dare raise their voices. We quietly retraced our steps back to the fork and on to the right track and on to C Company. I left them there and returned to BHQ. They didn't think much of me as a runner and guide.

As the days passed more and more people used the track past the privet bushes and more people looked over to the Tunnels. The enemy shelled the area twice one day. I had to go out with the signallers to repair damaged telephone wire on the track. From then on I kept well clear of the privet bushes. In fact I didn't hang round anywhere because Jap patrols moved around in the forests nearby. It was a very dangerous area.

A group of our chaps brought in a Japanese prisoner of war wounded in the leg. We gathered round to have a look at him. This was the first Jap prisoner of war we had seen in the three months we had been in action. He was a small man with a funny beard that went under his chin like a chinstrap, but with no hair above his mouth. He looked dirty and dusty as if he had been in action a long time, very different to the photos they carried of themselves, being neat, tidy and clean shaven in their uniform. The MO and orderlies had to clear us away and they offered him a cup of tea while the MO checked his leg. He didn't trust anyone and refused the tea. The 'I' Section Officer came to help the MO and decided to move him to a quieter place as many of the soldiers felt hostile towards him. He was sent further back to be looked after and questioned. He would be considered dead by Japanese Army Code for allowing him self to be captured.

Our advance through the Arakan had cost us a lot of men. They decided that fresh troops would finish the job. We had a lot of bad luck really and with victory of taking the Tunnels in sight, we were replaced. I wasn't sorry to leave those hit and miss journeys up and down that dodgy game trail and was glad to be going. On my last run, I didn't bother to look over the privet bushes that gave the unique view of the Jap held Tunnels but kept well down. I climbed over a four-foot high tree trunk, elephant manure and the watery elephant footprints of the assault course, over the slope, still following the telephone wire until I met that dummy wire that joined it. I didn't make the mistake of following the wrong trail this time. I stuck to the right hand trail that led me down to another part of the jungle river where my rifle company were dug in on the mountainside. I delivered my message and went back fast. These Jap infested rain forests were no place to look around. When I returned, I did take a quick last look at the Tunnels through the privet bushes. This was a Russian roulette kind of life that I had survived so far. To complete that last run gave some relief.

Fresh troops moved into our rifle company positions towards the end of March 1944 and what was left of our rifle company sections moved out. Our soldiers now had old men's faces, strained and tired under their tan. These were men that had lived a lifetime in a day, seen friends blown apart by shells doing impossible jobs. Nevertheless, we had advanced across and captured most of the Arakan up to the Tunnels. We'd been in action a little over three months, losing seventy men with over two hundred wounded.

Although we were now battle-hardened soldiers, little could prepare us for what we were about to face.

CHAPTER 3

We watched our wounded come down from the rainforests and ridges and saw friends that we knew on stretchers like 'Happy' Hamstead from Pershore. I knew him from training days in Worcester. "Alright Happy." I said, as he passed. He smiled weakly. He lay belly down on his stretcher while the MO checked his wounds. Happy had his back riddled with bullets from an enemy machine gun. It was over fifty years later that I learned that he'd survived.

We moved into the large deserted village of Kanyindan to regroup, together with mules and muleteers carrying supplies from Rear Admin. Some Sections were down to four men. We took over the huts, or bashas as we knew them. I remained with BHQ Signals platoon, retained as C Company runner. A big mule with a large radio set was unloaded for BHQ and company telephones and telephone wire was set up all over the village. Our radio operator was already at work, "I say again, Able, Baker, Charlie, Dog. Come in. Able, Baker, Charlie, Dog. Come in." He rattled persistently into the radio set as he tried to contact his rifle company's headquarters. We were allotted our huts. I shared mine with other signals runners, officers and batmen. Each of us had a bed space to unroll our bedding rolls, one blanket and a ground sheet, leaving our packs, ammunition pouches, water bottles, on top to mark our spot. We then got on with the business of settling into the camp. The cooks served dinner of dehydrated potatoes, tinned mutton, peas or beans and some kind of sweet, all washed down with a mug of tea which we all gratefully took back to our bashas. A few new replacements had arrived mostly Welsh. They all seemed to be called Williams, Morgan, Davies or Jones. We had beer that night to get to know them better ending in a hearty singsong. We were a good mix of Brummies, Welsh, Cockneys and Kentish men with the odd Irishman, Geordie and Black Country chap. There were also some Jewish lads with us. It was hard to tell that this area of jungle scrub, foothills and paddy fields was just behind the front line action except for the odd sound of the crack-pop of a Jap rifle or the loud bang of a shell burst now and then in the distance. We were back for a rest. We took things easy. Some got letters and parcels. I received a parcel of cigarettes and chocolate. As I opened mine I found that the chocolate bar had melted into a mass of silvery paper. I managed to eat a little and shared some, spitting out the silver paper as I ate. We got some extra airmail letters and cards to write home. That was a rarity as was the extra beer and food.

All the entertainment was brought with us. The pioneers would build a stage for any concerts or shows. We saw George and Beryl Formby at Dimapur. They persuaded Beryl to pose on the back of an elephant. She was scared but she did it. The elephant sat down and she slid off. Of course everyone erupted with laughter. She wasn't pleased at all. But we did appreciate these performers. They had some bottle to come out and entertain us. It wasn't that far behind the front line. George Formby brought seven banjos with him each tuned to a particular song. He'd dropped one and it was damaged. Ivan Daunt, one of the pioneers, repaired and glued it for him. It played perfectly. A screen was put up on a dried paddyfield for a film to be shown one night by a mobile film crew. It seems strange now, that on that moonlight night, just behind the front line, we sat and watched a film. We felt a little uneasy at first. The Japs had been known to shell these film shows as they lit up the area in the surrounding darkness. But we soon forgot about that and sat down and enjoyed a good film and then to bed for a good night's sleep. Bill Cordwell (we called him Ernie), a corporal from BHQ, saw some Japs in the bushes watching the film. They must have been a forward patrol and stumbled upon us. They didn't hang around and soon cleared off. One of our patrols tracked them down and sorted them out.

The next morning someone discovered a large inland lake a few hundred yards away. After breakfast a group of us decided to set off for a swim. We chatted about what a good time we would have cooling ourselves down in the oppressive heat. We stripped off and dashed towards the lake, naked like a crowd of eager school kids. We waded into the water and kept wading and wading, only to find that it was only a foot deep. It didn't get any deeper. Despite our disappointment, we made the most of it, splashing and cooling off.

I had nearly forgotten that I was still C Company Runner. I spent most of one day resting in the shade of our basha when the NCO called for me and explained that O (Operations) Group had asked all Officers to report to BHQ. I got that sinking feeling of dread for the future as I moved around to alert the Officers. After a few minutes, it was our turn to hear the bad news. We were to go back into action. We wrote our last letters home, starting "Dear Mom, If you don't hear from me in the next few weeks don't worry," together with a few silly excuses that fooled no one at home, but we felt it best to cloud the real issue and not to let them worry. We cleaned and fused our extra grenades, loaded extra Bren gun magazines and extra bandoliers of bullets, rations of food and moved out in company formation. We rode in trucks with some ex- grammar school chaps from I Section, well spoken and rather posh in our mind but good lads all the same. We had a singsong on the way to the airstrip. Then we filed onto the waiting Curtis Commandos. For many this was the first time on a plane. It wasn't a good advert for flying. It wasn't very comfortable. There weren't any seats. We had to sit on our packs. The crew were American. The navigator kept poking his head out telling us that if we saw any Japs to put the Bren guns out of the windows and shoot them. That didn't do much for our confidence. I couldn't see anything except trees and hills and more trees and hills. They had parachutes. We didn't. When we asked why, they said it was their plane! When we asked what we'd do if we had to bale out, the pilot said, 'You'll have to bale out won't you!' That wasn't much comfort. Tom Hogg went with the mules in British Dakotas. As soon as the engines roared into action they urinated everywhere. In the heat the stench was awful. The aircrew went mad. The urine collected beneath the floor of the fuselage amongst the electrics. I don't know how they got rid of it. It must have stunk for ages.

We landed at the flooded airstrip at Dimapur and were piled into trucks that headed up the winding hairpin road up the mountain range towards Kohima. We passed bewildered groups of Naga tribesmen; short sturdy hill people with a feather tied in their hair and a small pigtail near the nape of their neck. Many of them wore a red blanket on their shoulders and appeared to us more like the Red Indians than Asians. Some were carrying old shotguns. Others had spears or bows but all wore a Ghurkha style knife on their hips.

We reached Kohima and started to dig in. Then the order came saying that we weren't needed so after a few hours, we went back to a Dimapur. It was only a small place then but it was important with its railhead for supplies. There we were put on standby and told to make the most of our short rest. We didn't get long and were soon back on the trucks heading for Kohima. The air became cooler. Perhaps we would dispense with our mosquito nets at long last. But that was to be the least of our problems because as we got nearer we could see and hear shell bursts and mortar bombs and hear the crack-pop sound of the Japanese rifles. We noticed some Asian deserters running back shouting fanatically and throwing their weapons and bandoliers of bullets onto our trucks. We were angry when we saw them but were told there was a roadblock further on and they would be stopped and reorganised. We passed trucks coming back, packed with men, some hanging wherever they could. Others ran, trotted or walked. They all looked petrified. These were the non-combatants, store men, accountants and clerks.

It was 5th April 1944. The Japanese had launched an offensive. One hundred thousand men had crossed the Chindwin River in a big push to invade India. The military authorities had thought that it was impossible for the enemy to bring an army through the dense, disease-ridden jungle and mountains at any sustainable level, let alone in such massive numbers. The defences around Imphal, Dimapur and Kohima were apportioned accordingly. The Japs had surrounded Imphal and sent their 31st Division north to capture Dimapur and its airstrip. Between Imphal and Dimapur and astride the Japanese lines of communication was the small Garrison town of Kohima. The town itself was five thousand feet above sea level and set in a mountain range on the Indo-Burma border. The Japanese had to capture this town if they were to attack Dimapur.

Kohima was a forward supply depot and convalescent centre. It had its central point on a road junction between Dimapur and Imphal, a road that turned south and was joined by the Jessami Track. North of the centre, a steep track led to the ridge where a small wooden type Fort was positioned. The men dug in around near here and the position stretched down to a narrow spur towards the southeast housing the convalescence depot and other small tin roofed wooden huts. Further north among the trees was the Naga village overlooking the township. To the south lay the District Commissioner's (DC's) Bungalow with Tennis Court and what used to be beautifully maintained gardens. Continuing further south, along the spur

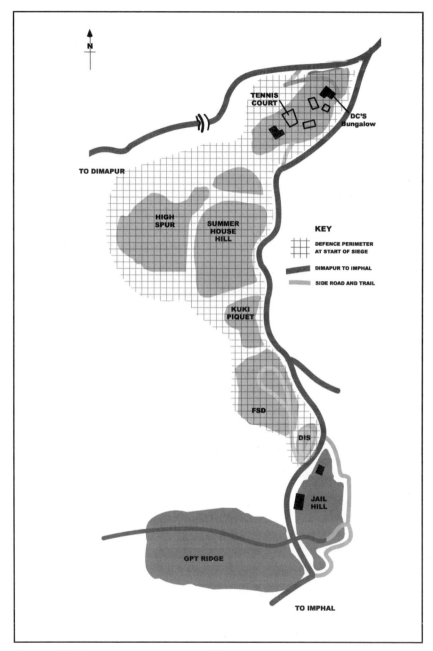

Map of Kohima at the beginning of the seige.

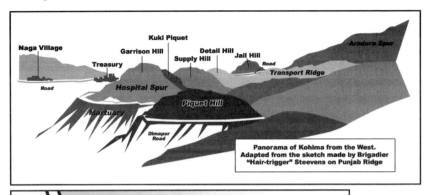

Panorama of Kohima from the West.
Adapted from the sketch made by Brigadier
"Hair-trigger" Steevens on Punjab Ridge

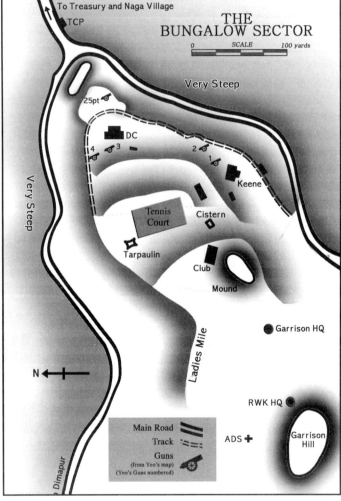

The Bungalow Sector looking NE

District Commissioner's Garden before.

District Commissioner's bungalow before.

was Summerhouse Hill and the IGH (Indian General Hospital) Spur. Beyond this were a series of ridges and hills; Kuki Picquet, FSD ridge (where the Field Supply Depot was built) and DIS (Daily Issue Supplies) Spur which ran down towards the main road. Across the road Jail Hill rose and to the right was another ridge named GPT (General Purposes Transport) Ridge. The whole area was covered with tall trees. The vegetation was sparse and thin in contrast with the dense jungles and paddy fields of the Arakan.

Our lorries pulled up in a line, nose to tail and the men spilled out, leaving the main equipment on the trucks. We started to dig in straight away. The battle was already in full swing. Jap guns from the Naga village were already causing problems. It was cloudy and misty when we got there so we got to our positions unhindered. But the cloud and mist lifted. No sooner had the trucks stopped than the shelling started, reducing some of the lorries to blazing wrecks. The Indian drivers ran off, back down the road where we had come from. The Garrison had one large gun, a twenty-five pounder, located by the District Commissioner's Bungalow. It tried to respond but only fired one or two rounds before the Japs took it out. A chap called Browning manned it. He got hit in the head. He survived the rest of the siege but was killed by a machine gun burst to the stomach right at the end when we were being evacuated. Some men made daring and dangerous trips to the lorries to get medical supplies and blankets which were in short supply from the start.

Almost four hundred and fifty of us Royal West Kents came up to Kohima. The others were delayed and by then the Japs had blocked the road, so they couldn't get in. None of us were older than thirty-two, apart from some of the officers and many of them were in their twenties. Some were younger than me and I'd just turned twenty-four. We were split into six companies: A, B, C, D, HQ and BHQ and detailed to particular areas of the Garrison. A Company under Major Tom Kenyon and HQ Company set up on Summerhouse Hill; B Company under Major John Winstanley on Kuki Piquet; C Company under Major Shaw on DIS Spur and D under the young Captain Donald Easten, on IGH Spur, to the west of Summerhouse Hill. I was C Company runner attached to Battalion Headquarters (BHQ). My Company was detailed to dig in on DIS Spur. The entire area was no more than eleven hundred by nine hundred and fifty yards at its maximum. The Japs were everywhere.

The Pioneer platoon under Major Harry Smith, a former school teacher, were part of HQ Company and set about constructing the Battalion Headquarters, cookhouse and organised the rest of the infrastructure that always appeared wherever we went. They consisted of tradesmen, bricklayers, carpenters and a plumber. Les Crouch, Bob Clinch and Ivan 'Angus' Daunt were among them. Ivan and Bob joined up at the same time, together with Jack Eves in July 1939 as militiamen. Ivan was granted a special wedding licence before they were shipped off to France. His son was three and a half before he saw him. Jack was a Colour Sergeant. He sorted out the cooks. He and Bob were good footballers and represented the regiment. They were good too. Their defensive capabilities would certainly be tested now. BHQ was set up between Summerhouse Hill and the District Commissioner's Bungalow in some old Garrison Headquarters' Bunkers, a little above the Colonel Hugh Richards, Headquarters. He was the Garrison Commander. Indian troops were pulling down bashas and huts to give them a better line of fire. It was early morning. Ron Clayton, D Company Runner and myself started digging in behind a tree. When we had finished, Ron wasn't happy with it and thought the tree didn't allow us enough field of fire and would give the Japs something to aim at, so we moved a little further up the hill and started digging again. I wasn't happy about it but went along with it despite the work we had already done. Afterwards we were worn out and lay in our trench to rest. Our redundant trench was in front of us now and beyond that a long curved trench, similar to those of the First World War. This housed the cookhouse with its defences to the right. We runners were a few yards higher up, in three slit trenches. Behind us, in a big long bunker, was the Signals HQ under the command of the Signals Platoon Officer. Ernie

Douglas Short, John Steddy, Donald Easten, Tom Kenyon, Tom Coath, 'Tops' Topham and Fred Collett

Captain Topham, John Laverty, Major Franklin and Captain Short

Mason, B Company's radio operator was in there busily testing his equipment to make contact with his company. A little further back and to our right, towards Summerhouse Hill, was the BHQ Command Post. In the pine trees alongside us an armoured car lay on its side, its weapon missing and huge wheels motionless. Two chaps were detailed to smash it up later and pushed it into the adjacent nullah so it was out of the way. The whole area had become cratered with small shell holes and the litter and rancid smell of past warfare filled the air.

Our Commanding Officer was Lieutenant-Colonel John Laverty. The men called him 'Texas Dan' because of his tall lean build and his hat. He always carried a six foot bamboo staff to negotiate steep and rocky ground. His batman was Private Heffernan. They were Irish and good friends. They were a right pair of characters. Heffernan always greeted everybody with, "Top o' the morning to you." The CO had to pull rank on many occasions to shut him up. On arrival, lines of communication were set up to all the companies and Major Yeo of 24th Indian Mountain Battery could now direct his artillery at nearby Jotsoma from his position within the Garrison.

The enemy sent over barrages of shells that continued into the night and again the next day. Joe Walsh, an Irish kid, was the first of our mob to killed there. One shell slammed down into our former trench behind the tree. This was too close for comfort, so we de-

Colonel Laverty

cided to dig deeper and bottle out the bottom on the trench so that we could both lie flat side by side. I looked out of my trench and a chap that was standing in the doorway of a hut near the water tank suddenly disappeared as a shell exploded in front of him. The Jap guns must have been very near because you couldn't hear the shells coming. We called them 'whizz-bangs' because that's how they sounded. We only just had time to throw ourselves down as the shells screamed down on us. The tree bursts were worst. The shrapnel would ricochet amongst the branches and rain down into the trenches below. Some of the troops used timber and the corrugated metal sheet off the bashas topped with soil to give head cover, but they couldn't do that in the forward trenches. They had to be ready for the Jap infantry attacks. Some Indians near us left their trenches and made an open fire, but the smoke drew more shellfire and scattered them quickly back into their trenches. They didn't do that again. One chap was a bike rider and kept his motorbike in the long curved trench by BHQ. It was virtually brand new and I suppose he didn't want it damaged in the barrages. However, someone fell over it and chucked it out and it was damaged in the next barrage. The rider was furious and laid into the chap who'd thrown it out. They were having a right set to when a NCO broke them up saying that we had enough problems sorting the Japs let alone fighting amongst ourselves. He could have put them on a charge but there was no point in that.

The morning of 6th April was sunny after a misty start. The mist was thick and damp. You could only see for about thirty yards. As the temperature rose the mist condensed and fell like rain from the surrounding trees, soaking everyone. The trees were beautiful pines, lantanas, oaks and alders but it wouldn't be long until all their foliage would be blasted away and their trunks and branches split and splintered beyond recognition. In the early morning, the Japs had taken Jail Hill and GPT Ridge. D Company tried to retake it but there were too many of them, so they consolidated and dug in at FSD. This was a blow because now the Japs were above us and could see C Company's positions on DIS, although the tree cover helped at first. I had to run messages to them and was exposed to enemy fire. There was very little cover. The Japs made the most of their position and fully established themselves on Jail Hill with extensive tunnels, some of which were extended with underground galleries, safe from the heaviest artillery and aircraft shells.

Most of my day was spent organising and collecting mortar bombs and other ammunition that had been stacked near the roadside by the trucks. It was a hell of a job, Jap snipers were firing at us. Some Rajputs arrived, sent by Brigade HQ. They were sent immediately to DIS and dug in with the rest. They were the last troops to get through. The Japs had closed the road and we were under siege. The telephone cable lasted a further six hours before the Japs cut it. A detachment of 75th Indian Field Ambulance had got through, commanded by Lieutenant-Colonel John Young, a fair, slight, wiry built man that immediately took control of the disjointed medical facilities. He organised the construction of an Advanced Dressing Station (ADS) near BHQ, to replace the five scattered Dressing Stations. There were lots of casualties before he got there. The hospital buildings were already overflowing. Something had to be done. Lieutenant-Colonel Young could speak fluent Urdu and that was important in the ADS. With a chap called Barrett of the 1/17 Dogras 123 Brigade, 5th Indian Division, they organised some of the Indians and non-combatants to construct the ADS and do other jobs such as digging trenches to house the wounded and also bury the dead. This allowed some of the fighting men to remain in their positions.

The Japs soon realised that we were there and not going to move. From then on their attacks became more intense. The 4th Royal West Kent Regiment held the main perimeter areas. Other troops helped defend the Garrison: the Assam regiment; Assam Rifles; A Company of 4/7th Rajputs; 20th Indian Mountain Battery; a platoon of 2nd Field Company, King George V Sappers and Miners; 75th Indian Field Ambulance plus other odds and sods. These odds and sods, as they were called, were soldiers from mixed units, some from the convalescent or rest camps at the Garrison, now trapped here with us. Also trapped were the non-combatants. These were clerks, store men and other administrative staff. They weren't trained for action and a burden. Some of them were very scared. They had good reason to be. We all were. There were nearly fifteen thousand Japs out there. We numbered a little over a thousand fighting men. 'Invicta' was our regimental motto. It meant 'Unconquered.' Things didn't look good. The Unconquered were about to have their sternest test ever.

George Martin's Grave

That night the Japs directed a full-scale attack on C Company on DIS Spur, commencing with a barrage from behind some buildings on Jail Hill. George Martin was killed when a mortar landed on his position. DIS was a supply point, a small oval feature extending to about one

Victor King

hundred and sixty yards in length and about thirty to forty yards wide in the middle. The bashas still housed plentiful stocks of food and provisions together with ammunition. C Company occupied trenches, their position was some twenty yards wide at the southern edge overlooking Jail Hill, separated by the macadam Imphal Road. Major Shaw made us remove the overhead cover to the trenches to improve our field of fire. After the barrage stopped the Jap infantry attacked. They didn't make a secret of it. The moon was out and we could clearly see them forming up on Jail Hill. The Japs made a hell of a racket, blowing bugles, screaming and shouting, psyching themselves up for the charge. There was no doubt about it, we were scared. Then the training kicked in. We saw them come down Jail Hill and start to cross the road approaching the steep climb to our positions. We held our fire till then. They were about thirty yards away when we let them have it. Artillery back up from Major Yeo's 24th Mountain Battery guns were directed at the oncoming Japs, together with Sergeant Victor King's mortars. Roy Wellings, a corporal in 13 Platoon of C Company was in one of the forward trenches and Victor King dropped in to get the 'lay of the land.' Wellings crept forward five yards, in the darkness, to the edge of the slope to spot the fall of King's ranging shots. King then phoned through to give the mortars their bearings. They were very accurate and had a devastating affect, killing and maiming many of the enemy as they charged. But they kept coming, wave after wave of them, rushing towards our trenches. We used rifles and grenades plus the Bren guns. We cut them to ribbons but they still got through. There was that many of them. Roy Wellings couldn't fire quickly enough. Despite hitting as many as possible, he was overrun. They ran past him towards the trenches beyond. He thought they might shoot him in the back but he couldn't look round. He didn't have time. He just continued firing and hoped those behind would deal with the others. They did and the position was held. The Japs withdrew to regroup. Despite their losses they attacked again and again. At one stage Roy fell back and was bayoneting vertically as the Japs ran over his position. It was all he could do. Major Shaw, our Company commander was hit in the leg after a tree burst by HQ. Privates Young and Sharpe were also hit. Not only wounded, Shaw's leg was broken in several places. Corporal Day, one of the stretcher-bearers, took him to a basha and Captain 'Dodo' Watts took over. During the night, some Japs were heard digging in near to 13 Platoon. There were about one hundred of them and they were only yards away. Led by Sergeant Tacon, with covering fire from Corporal Norman, Privates Dick Johnson and Ernie Thrussel, a group with small arms and grenades attacked and wiped them out. Corporal Webber was with them. His section killed loads. There was a lot of action around HQ. Captain Watts was injured in the arm and taken to the ADS. Liddell and Woodward were wounded, but Ginger Judges one of the cooks wasn't so lucky. He was killed. Privates Frank Bennett and Alan Paris were also killed that day. Throughout the action Sergeant Stammers constantly visited his section posts topping up their ammunition and giving words of encouragement to the men.

Some Japs got into bashas housing ammunition stores in the middle of our position further up towards the top of DIS. They must have sneaked round the west flank. We couldn't direct the artillery on to them in case they hit our blokes, so it was decided to wait until the next day to sort them out. When the rest of the Japs finally withdrew the hillside was littered with hundreds of dead enemy corpses, too many to count. Our losses weren't light. Jimmy Beames was in Roy Wellings' 13 Platoon. He caught a bullet in the shoulder but stayed at his post instead of going to the ADS. We couldn't afford to keep winning like this. We didn't have the men. It was hard to bury the dead. The Japs sniped us and the ground was so hard to dig, you couldn't get very deep. Rigor mortis set in and parts of arms and legs would poke out of the shallow graves. We buried them at night. They left their dead until they captured the position and then burnt them. The smell of dead and burning flesh was terrible and drifted across our lines. During the night they tried 'jitter tactics' to try and identify where we were. They would shout, "Let me through. The Japs are after me." No one replied. They even got snipers to fire single shots here and there and awaited any response to try to assess the strength of our guns. We didn't take the bait.

There was a water tank close to my trench, a little way down the hill towards the Tennis Court. At least we would be all right for water and that was a relief when I remembered what it was like at times in the Arakan.

We had water for two days before the Japs shelled it. It was only then that someone decided to cover it with some camouflage netting. The water was still flowing through the pipe, but that only lasted a few more days before the Japs captured the reservoir nearby and turned the supply off completely. From then on water was rationed and thirst became a problem.

The shelling became more regular; the Japs letting us have a barrage at first light and then at dusk, always followed by frenzied infantry attacks on the forward positions. We were lucky where we were, but the troops in the front line were involved in hand-to-hand combat each time they attacked. It was calmer during the day, but we still had to be on the lookout for snipers and isolated machine gun and mortar fire. We had to be careful all the time. On one occasion we were sent scattering to the bottom of our trenches as a Jap machine gun swept our area with indirect fire. It didn't last long. I don't think he had any particular target in mind but was firing indiscriminately hoping to catch us off guard. He nearly did. In a quieter moment, I looked around and saw some poor tethered mules eating hay or straw with large open wounds in their flanks. They didn't seem to be distressed. They munched steadily at their hay but later that day they had gone. I hoped that someone had cut them free.

The runs I had to make were different now. For a start they were shorter and would become shorter each day as the Japs pushed us back. I had to take messages in the dark. It was too dangerous in daylight. Whilst taking one message at night, I followed a track over the back of our hill through Kuki Piquet down FSD ridge to DIS Spur. The sound of someone digging close by alerted me so I slowed down, but it was too late. I was suddenly challenged by a voice, "Halt." "Friend." I quickly replied. The voice in the shadows growled, "Password." My mind went blank. The password was 'Chowringee,' It suddenly came back to me and I said it quietly but eagerly, as to hesitate over a password could mean death. I reminded them that I would be coming back that way but their faces said it all. Make sure we hear you and you know the password or else you're dead. As it happened, these soldiers had just had a hard time, so I couldn't blame them. They were digging a grave for a dead friend and were on edge. It was as well I answered quickly for they were in no mood for anyone like me playing silly beggars. The passwords used at Kohima often used the letter L, such as 'Lollypop' or 'Lilliput' as it was thought the Japs would have problems

Aerial View of Kohima

with their pronunciation. This would help the guards especially in the dark. Also some of the radio operators would talk in Welsh in case the Japs were listening. They were sure they wouldn't understand that. On one of the following runs, I noticed a case of whisky fastened by a padlock lying on the ground. I passed it but didn't touch it. Someone else did. When I went by the next day the case had been broken open and the lot had gone.

As the enemy tightened their grip, we were pinned down. We hadn't had a haircut for ages and because of the water situation were unable to wash or shave. We were always thirsty. We used an old fruit tin for urine and threw the contents over the parapet. We used our old redundant shell holed trench for a toilet whenever we could. The whole area began to stink. During the night we got a shower of rain and caught about a pint of water in an old gas cape. We managed to get it into a container, but it was so bitter and the taste of rubber made it so sickly, that we couldn't drink it for the fear that we would make ourselves ill. Disappointed, we returned to our trench. Luckily we were sitting down when some Japanese machine gun fire swept our position again. I felt that our trench was taking the brunt of it as the bullets zipped above us and into our parapet. This went on for a few minutes, but we kept our heads low for the next hour or two just in case. For three nights running, a Japanese mobile gun had been sending shellfire on to our position. We would hear him approach, stop, fire his shells, then start up again, move to another position to fire at us again. He was on a road somewhere nearby and would keep moving so that our artillery couldn't get a bearing on him. This became nerve racking as the engine turned over and then suddenly stopped. We knew that we'd soon hear the screaming sound of the shells. We immediately hit the bottom of the trench for cover. Each attack lasted for about half an hour.

7th April was Good Friday. We used to have hot-cross buns at home. Here it was bully beef and biscuits. During the morning D Company were detailed to assist with the removal of the Japs from the bashas amongst C Company, aided by a platoon of sappers. If they couldn't get them out C Company would be cut off, overrun and killed and DIS taken. It was that serious. The area concerned included several bashas, one of which was a bakery. Tree cover made observation difficult and the Japs had positioned some 75 mm guns on the recently occupied GPT Ridge. Lieutenant Peter Doresa was in charge of a platoon sent to the northeast of DIS to help clear the Japs from the occupied bashas. Major Donald Easten set up a covering crossfire from some Bren guns, Sergeant Major Haines, led the platoon, plus some Ghurkhas, on a forty-yard dash uphill to the Jap occupied bashas. With bayonets fixed and throwing grenades they went straight into the enemy positions. Some bashas caught fire as the ammunition and explosives inside went off. Some Japs stayed inside fighting until they burnt to death. Others ran out, some with their clothes on fire and were cut down by Bren and rifle fire or by bayonet during the hand-to-hand combat that took place. Sergeant Tacon manned a Bren further down the slope. As the fleeing Japs came down they came to the edge of a terrace. They slowed and hesitated and had to jump down. He mowed them down and heaps of their dead littered the area. Later CSM Bert Harwood came over to see Tacon and was amazed that he had a little white dog with him in his trench. He didn't know were he'd got it. He didn't care. He had enough to worry about and left him to it.

Ivan Daunt, one of the pioneers and some others from HQ Company and some of the odds and sods were deployed to assist C Company in positions overlooking the main road. The Japs sent some shells over and yellow smoke started to work its way up the hill. Some of the odds and sods thought it was mustard gas and ran off. It wasn't. Later, there was a loud rumble and a number of horses and mules galloped past immediately followed by screaming and shouting Japs. If the galloping animals were supposed to divert our attention the noise the Japs made didn't conceal anything. In any event, the liberal use of grenades and small arms fire stopped their progress.

The bashas were of bamboo construction with thatched or corrugated metal roofs but the bakery was built of brick around the ovens. The Japs used boxes and crates to construct defences and were well established. Due to the trees, shrubbery and other huts they proved difficult to remove. They fired from between the crates and boxes and positioned a machine gun in the Bakery doorway overlooking C Company positions. They had also captured some Indian troops and forced them to fire on us. The weakest point was the eastern face but that was where the brick ovens were. So, Lieutenant John Wright in charge of the sappers and Donald Easten in charge of D Company, fixed bales of gun cotton to an old door taken from the Hospital, fused and charged it and ran up the hill towards the bakery. They wedged the door against the brick ovens ignited the fuse and ran back to their position. A terrific explosion took place with bricks, timber, metal and provisions flying everywhere. The Japs ran out through the dust and smoke and were immediately cut down by C Company with Brens and rifles. There was some close quarter fighting as they desperately tried to flee. Easten just managed to shoot one Jap with his revolver as he got within a couple of yards of him. Nearly fifty Japs were killed. Not many escaped and if they did they were certainly all wounded. Some of our chaps saw a wounded Jap fall as he was running off and went to take him in. As they approached he pulled the pin from a grenade and blew himself to pieces wounding and killing some of his would be captors. We had further losses with Privates John Coleman and Joe Hesketh killed. They were both young kids. Hesketh being one of the youngest amongst us at nineteen. After some close quarter resistance, two Jap prisoners were taken, the first ones to be captured here. They were both badly wounded. The officer had a broken leg and died later. The corporal lived a little over a week. Because of the disgrace in being captured, he willingly submitted information. Although there was no Jap interpreter, the Intelligence Officer somehow got details of the Jap positions and strength of numbers.

John Harman (some of us called him Jack) was D Company sniper and pretty damn good too. As a soldier he was first rate, very brave. It was him who carried 'Happy' Hamstead to safety when he was shot by a Jap machine gun. 'Happy' was one of the few who got close to him. He told 'Happy' that he had maps of sunken Spanish galleons in the Bristol Channel and suggested they hunt for treasure when the war was over. It was rumoured that he was offered a commission but preferred to be one of the lads. That was strange really because he was a natural leader but also a bit of a loner. Although everyone got on with him, he was

John Harman

too posh for most. Don't get me wrong he wasn't a snob. You see his father was a multimillionaire. He owned Lundy Island. He was different to us. They even had their own coins and stamps. John was older than most, nearly thirty, well travelled and well read. We'd be lucky to go to Rhyl for a day out but he'd travelled the world. He had worked as a lumberjack in New Zealand and had done sheep farming in Australia. There wasn't much he didn't know. I first met him at Market Rasen at the training camp. He was with us at Allahabad when we came to India. I remember when we were travelling on the train across India; we would guess where we were. He knew. He had his own maps and compass and already had worked out where we were and where we were going. He didn't make a fuss about it. It was a matter of fact to him. He was the only bloke I knew who had a bank account set up in India. His father set it up for him so he wouldn't go short. He even had his boots specially made. Some people said he had odd sized feet and made up a pair to fit from two Japs he'd killed. I don't know about that but 'Happy' gratefully accepted a pair after John had decided he needed a change and he said they were all right. But he was superstitious. Apparently he'd had his fortune read in Spain before the war and was told that he would live until he was seventy. 'Happy' was with him in Durban on the voyage out. John visited a Portuguese woman for a reading and once more was told that he would live a long life. One of our NCOs called Edmonds was with him at the hill station at Raniket when Harman asked an Indian fortuneteller to read his hand. But when the Indian looked he was visibly shaken and immediately got up and walked off refusing to read any more.

Ivan Daunt knew him well and had some right banter with him. Harman dropped in for a chat one time on the Arakan. He shouldn't have been there. It was nowhere near his company position. He was always where he shouldn't have been. Ivan teased him about his father owning Lundy Isle as his family lived in Starkey Castle, in Kent. They didn't own it. They rented it, but Harman didn't know that. They talked about food or rather the lack of it when Harman asked if they fancied some rice. They said, 'yes,' and Harman disappeared for a short time and returned with two sacks of rice. He'd found them in a redundant Jap foxhole on one of his walkabouts.

Despite his straightforward approach, there was a bit of the rogue in him. It was on the trip to Raniket that he looked over the sheer drop at the edge of the road and saw the tail of a snake. Without hesitation he immediately grabbed the reptile's tail and pulled it out of the crevice and shook it to death. He then paid a local Indian to make him a belt from the skin. On another occasion at Allahabad he caught a rock python, brought it into the barracks and let it wrap itself around some chap's bedpost. Then he woke him up. Well, as you can imagine the chap went to pieces with panic. Harman simply grabbed the snake's tail and with a whip-like action rendered it harmless. Another belt was made from the proceeds. He certainly had no fear of these creatures or indeed any other animal. In fact he was quite at home with them. On Lundy he kept hives of bees and was always out and about, happiest amongst the nature of the island. In India it was much the same. He'd often disappear on his own and go for a walk, even in the terrific heat of the midday sun. In the Arakan he would go out and return with chapattis or some other local produce that he had bartered for with the local natives. On one occasion he returned with a young water buffalo. He thought a bit of steak would make a nice change for the lads. It did.

There was some talk of trying to get a patrol through to us from our own brigade outside Kohima, but the Jap roadblocks held everyone up. During the night, despite the shortage of fighting men, the Rajputs were withdrawn. However, they took over ninety of the walking wounded out with them together with about one hundred of the non-combatants. They had been wandering about, in the way and bad for morale. Major Peter Franklin and Lieutenant Colonel John Young, the MO, led them out. Ivan Daunt and some others went with them to help but had to come back afterwards. We hoped they'd tell others of an unguarded way in. It didn't happen, but they got back safely without loss. Straight after this we were finally cut off and surrounded. There was now no way in or out for our troops. The remaining wounded lay in long crawl trenches as the sick bay overflowed. They were in an awful state. Barrett and his Indians and other non-combatants dug more trenches for the injured, but they couldn't get very deep. After about two feet they hit rock and that wasn't deep enough to protect them during the shelling and many got wounded again or killed because of the lack of head cover. They had more luck with the operating theatres. They constructed two and managed to get to six feet in one place. One with a timber roof and one just covered by a tarpaulin. Both were lit by hurricane lamps. It wasn't good enough but it was all they had. As soon as they were finished the doctors started to operate with trestles and stretchers serving as operating tables. When Barrett's men had finished digging the trenches, they would help nurse the sick and wounded, removing the dead from amongst them and then took up the stretchers to bring new cases in. They were great. When rations were scarce, they gave up theirs for the wounded. When water was short, the wounded were given fruit or tomato juice just to get fluid into them. They couldn't do without. Barrett's men were very brave. They had to go all the way to DIS to get supplies, constantly under threat of fire from the enemy. Later, usually at night they would help bury the dead. This had to be done quickly due to the accelerated decomposition in the heat. Both the Japs and our blokes were buried together. There wasn't time to sort them out. Details of our dead were taken, hopefully to be sorted out afterwards. It was. They had a hell of a game burying the mules. The ground was so hard, but it had to be done. They couldn't be left to rot. Flies were everywhere.

With Captain Watts injured, Captain Tom Coath assumed command of C Company. We all liked him. Despite being an officer he seemed one of the lads. Ivan Daunt knew him before the war. He was a salesman, a great rugby player too. On the boat out to the Middle East there was a rumour that Tom couldn't afford his mess fees. He was that well respected that the men had a whip round to help out.

The Japs attacked DIS that night, mainly jitter and probing tactics to assess the strength of our positions. The attacks were hourly so no one got any sleep. They knew what they were doing. Yeo organised the outside artillery to fire on to the Japs as they formed up to attack. That helped. Roy Wellings was in a trench near the edge of the road. The chap beside him was already dead. He heard a noise but couldn't see anything in the darkness. There was a drop to the road below, so he half pitched and half rolled a grenade down the slope. As it exploded he saw the faces of the Japs that had been creeping up on him. The grenade put paid to their attack.

On the morning of the 8th April we woke to be greeted by a machine gun that the Japs had managed to get onto DIS during the night. This was serious as it could cover the whole of DIS and had the whole of C Company pinned down. We couldn't attack or fire on it effectively because of its position and the nature of the ground. It was only forty yards away. We'd suffer many casualties if we withdrew. Harman went out alone, first crawling before standing and running at the machine gun nest. The Japs saw him and fired continuously at him, but miraculously the bursts of machine gun fire went over his head. He reached the bunker entrance, pulled the pin from his grenade and let go of the clip. They only had a four second fuse. He counted aloud and as he said, "Three," he lobbed the grenade into the Jap position and dropped for cover. It immediately exploded. He jumped up and ran round into the bunker, checked the Japs were dead and returned back to his position with the machine gun to the cheers of the men. By mid morning the Japs had secured positions in the Fort and up the road at the Traffic Control Point (TCP). Jiffs (Japanese Indian Fighting Force) had occupied the bazaar and enemy artillery positioned on North and GPT Ridges could reach any part of the Garrison. Our own guns at Jotsoma weren't big enough to reach them so they had a free hand. That evening the Jap guns gave Summerhouse Hill, a terrible pounding, the worst to date. All the shells seemed to be directed at my trench. At the same time the Japs attacked C Company from Jail Hill. Again it was with wave after wave of fanatical, screaming troops. It was the heaviest attack so far. We cut them to ribbons but they kept coming.

They lost hundreds but it didn't deter them. Each attack was with fresh troops. They didn't seem to care. They were eventually driven back but we'd lost some ground and the Japs were gaining positions among us. We could have done with some barbed wire to make defensive entanglements. That would've slowed them down but there was none to be had.

Most of the shrubbery and small vegetation had gone under the enemy bombardment. The trees were heavily scarred and were losing their leaves where branches had been blasted away. Some were just spiked trunks now. Still the little red and yellow finches came back and perched on the jagged remains. The enemy continued their regime of shelling at dawn and dusk. We called the latter 'Evening Hate' They never let us down. They didn't discriminate either. Shells fell around the ADS killing nearly forty, most already wounded. The tree bursts did the most damage. Snipers were getting among us. They were in the trees, hidden amongst the leaves. You couldn't see them. They picked people off at will. Some used 'dum-dum' bullets. These exploded on impact causing severe injury. Our company sniper was called Cousins. He was red hot. He bagged seventeen Japs in one day. On one occasion he must have shot a sniper twenty times. He thought he had missed and was losing his touch, until he realised the Jap was already dead. He'd tied himself to the tree so didn't fall out. Somehow a sniper had made it onto the hill and was in a tree behind BHQ. He swept the area with automatic fire. Heffernan, the CO's batman calmly took his rifle and shot him first time. He was tied to the tree and his body lay hanging there for the rest of the siege.

There was no twilight. It was either daylight or night time, so when darkness came it was all of a sudden. Well, it was pitch black that night. There was no moonlight to help us out. It was terrible for those in the front line trenches. They could hear the Japs shuffling about but couldn't see anything only shapes and they couldn't be certain what they were. They could've been anything. Our eyes played tricks on us then, especially when we were that tired. If you fired and it wasn't anything it could give your position away or provoke an attack. It would at least lead to everyone standing to, so there would be no chance of any rest for those lucky enough to have a comrade left alive sharing the trench to keep lookout. During the night they attacked again, but this time it was different. They found out where our mortars were and concentrated their artillery on these positions reducing their effect. The Jap infantry charges were now more difficult to defend and they exploited this by gaining positions here and there. The usual barrage preceded them but they also used grenade launchers that gave the impression they were closer than they actually were. These were hand held and they set them off in showers with devastating effect. They attacked the District Commissioner's Bungalow area twice, the first from the Fort area, the second at the road junction adjacent to the Bungalow. They suffered massive losses but, unfortunately for us, managed to get small footholds on the Bungalow side of the road by the formerly immaculately maintained gardens. The beautiful rhodedendrons and other flowers and shrubs had disappeared. The bright red tiled roof was broken and smashed. The Japs capitalised on their gains straight away and reinforcements poured in as they prepared for the next attack. They even used one of our captured 3.7-inch guns against us. Some soldiers manned a Bren as they withdrew back to the Tennis Court terrace. They were told to hold to the last round. They did and after a heroic stance that secured the withdrawal, they were overrun, bayoneted and shot. Another chap pretended to be dead and had a very frightening time lying doggo as Japs walked and trampled over what they assumed to be his dead body. He couldn't make a sound or movement. They'd have killed him if they'd found out. He managed to escape the next day by running back through the mist to our lines. He was shot in the foot for his trouble by one of our men mistaking him for a Jap, but he was all right and gave us some very useful information about the Japs, their strength and positions. The Japs moved up to the chainlink fence on the east side of the Tennis Court. Some of A Company, led by Sergeant Brooks, were detailed to help the mixed units of troops already there. They dug in to the rear of the District Commissioner's Bungalow, around the Tennis Court about twenty yards from the enemy and around the Garrison Telephone Exchange. We could see the Japs digging in but dare not attack. We weren't ready then and there were too many of them. Sergeant Brooks and his men dug in by the Clubhouse and Mound on the terrace to the rear where a Bren was set up with a good field of fire. Lieutenant Hinton with his platoon dug in on the other flank with Major Tom Kenyon and his men in between. Movement on the Tennis Court was restricted due to both sides being so close to each other. Both the Japs and ourselves used grenades. No-one could move. We had to wait. The Japs mounted a third attack of the night at IGH on some mixed troops from the convalescent depot and rest camp and the Japs forced them to withdraw despite strong resistance.

C Company didn't have a quiet night either. Around midnight they heard Japs digging in. A couple of hours later an enemy mortar opened fire. Its rapid fire rained shells on them. This was the worst mortaring to date, especially in the forward trenches, which took a hell of a battering. One shell landed in a weapon pit killing Lieutenant Phythian's Batman, a chap called Walters. He took the brunt of the blast, falling on to his superior officer. This saved Phythian's life. He received minor leg wounds. The Japs attacked after the barrage but with the aid of the Indian guns on Jotsoma Ridge they were repelled again suffering great losses. Unfortunately one of the Indian guns put a shell down into a weapon pit occupied by Corporal Rees and two privates, Wells and Skingsley. Wells was killed. Rees and Skingsley were buried but managed to dig themselves out and moved to an adjacent trench. The Jap infantry attacked again with two hundred fresh troops and again they were mown down. They used grenade launchers and two landed in a Bren gun pit killing the gunner, Allchin. It was so difficult to see them in the darkness and pouring rain. Despite their casualties, the enemy were making some headway because of our lack of firepower from the trenches to stop them. There was some hideous hand-to-hand fighting. C Company were in a precarious position as Jail Hill was swarming with Japs and their snipers were picking our men off. They could clearly see many of our positions and it was impossible to put your head over the parapet of the trench in daylight without fear of having it blown off. Men got hit and there was no way to help them. They were left to die.

The Japs attacked DIS again. The front line only extended twenty yards. We couldn't improve things because the Japs on Jail Hill fired at anything that moved. Roy Wellings had a near miss when some shrapnel from one of the shells passed across his back and through his clothing. It even cut through his 'supply' of toilet paper that he kept tucked down his back, but he didn't get so much as a scratch on him. After the initial barrage, the Japs ran up the hill, screaming and shouting. Victor King's mortars helped take some out. They were very accurate and must have killed dozens but they still kept coming. When they got within range the Brens and rifles opened up, cutting them down in their droves but some got through, finally being shot a yard or two from the Bren gun positions. Despite their horrific losses the Japs attacked again and again and managed to take some of the forward trenches. No one retreated. They fought until they were killed. The Japs were only twenty-five yards from C Company's second line. Tom Greatley was only eighteen then. He'd joined up when he was sixteen. He was a big kid and looked a lot older. He went to the local police station. They asked him his age and he told them he was eighteen. He thought he would be found out when he reported to the barracks but no one said anything and that was that. He was with two other privates Lockyer and Lewis, in a bunker with a steep, vertical drop, about twelve feet, to the adjacent road below. Tom was on guard while the others tried to get what rest they could. He was priming and fusing his grenades when he heard noises on the road below. He woke his mates and had a look to see what was going on. The Japs had crept up with muffled weapons and wore plimsolls so they wouldn't be heard. They put a bamboo ladder up against the side of the bunker and started to make their way up. Tom took his grenades and dropped them over the side killing the Japs.

The District Commissioner's Bungalow and surrounding area was situated on the lower slopes of Summerhouse Hill on a narrow strip of stepped terraces projecting to the northeast, enclosed by the hairpin bend of the Imphal to Dimapur Road. A track called the Ladies Mile ran parallel to the road, presumably used by the colonials in more peaceful times to enjoy the picturesque views in the cooler mountain air. From the road a short macadam drive led to the bungalows of District Commissioner Pawsey and Lieutenant Colonel Keene with the kitchens and servants' quarters behind, on the terrace above. Behind these and nearly forty feet higher was another terrace that housed an asphalt Tennis Court with a large tarpaulin water tank at one corner and a larger steel water tank near the other end, on a lower slope. To the west of the Tennis Court another terrace rose seven or eight feet overlooking the court but the north and south elevations fell steeply forming the hairpin of the road below. Beyond this terrace was another terrace where a small social clubhouse was built. Within the same terrace was a mound, about seventy by twenty feet, a distinctive feature of great tactical importance as it looked over most of the eastern lower slopes. It was constructed of surplus material left after one of the lower terraces had to be flattened to create a parade area. All the terraces were steep and you couldn't see anything below unless you were near the edge so when the Japs attacked you could only see them when they came over the top.

The 9th April was Easter Sunday - no Easter eggs for us. It wasn't very happy either. It rained and was cold. The Padre held the Easter Sunday service in the ADS. Only twelve attended. We tried to clear the Japs off IGH Spur and, although we pushed them back, they still held on to some positions. A Company counter attacked the Japs at the District Commissioner's Bungalow but couldn't shift them. Later that day the rest of A company were sent down to the Bungalow area to dig in and reinforce the defences.

Our situation was getting worse, especially with the shortage of water and medical supplies. The enemy had cut off the water some days ago and it was only available from a few places such as small streams or a joint on the mains pipe. These were all under the noses of the Japs and could only be used at night. We were rationed to three quarters of a pint a day. That was nothing in those conditions and thirst became a big problem. The growing number of wounded was exhausting the medical supplies. The previous night John Young, the MO, went out with some Indian sappers to the 53 IGH and to our lorries to get some blankets and any medicines that were available. They were very brave but encountered no Japs and brought back what they could. Evacuation of the wounded wasn't an option and so the shallow crawl trenches were extended. The doctors did what they could. It was terrible when, after they had patched them up, they were re-wounded or killed by enemy shells as they lay in the crawl trenches.

Donald Easten had already brought up some men to assist C Company and among these was John Harman. Just after first light, Easten noticed that the Japs were reworking one of C Company's old trenches, converting it to a machine gun pit to fire on our troops. Harman decided to attack it himself. He ordered his Bren gunner, to cover him and moved from his trench and ran down the hill and through the trees towards the machine gun nest making no use of the little cover available. Alec Haughton another private in D Company saw him go and used his Bren to give supporting fire from further up the hill. Harman went from side to side searching for the best position to overlook the enemy. The Japs wildly shooting back at him. He stopped a few yards in front of their position and, firing his rifle from the hip, shot four of them before jumping into the weapon pit bayoneting the fifth and making sure the others were dead. He reappeared holding the machine gun aloft and smashed it into the ground in front of everybody. Cheers went up from the surrounding soldiers at such a heroic deed but John simply climbed up the ridge and walked back, despite shouts from his comrades to run. Just before he reached safety, a

Japanese machine gun from Jail Hill caught him below the spine. Easten ran out and pulled him back. He refused treatment and died a few minutes later. For this and previous action he was posthumously awarded the Victoria Cross for his bravery. Back on Lundy Isle, all his bees mysteriously and suddenly died.

Corporal Trevor 'Taffy' Rees stood up to watch Harman's action from the edge of his weapon pit. Unfortunately, he didn't realise that the Japs had fixed line machine guns on that position and he was hit, falling into a dip a couple of yards away. Sergeant Tacon tried to get him back but was shot in the arm and the leg for his trouble but managed to roll back into his position. Poor Rees was paralysed and no one could help him. He went delirious, screamed in pain and prayed aloud. He called for his wife Margaret, his Mom and Dad. Tom Coath tried to set up a smoke screen so that the stretcher-bearers could get to him but it was no good, the Japs knew what we were up to and saturated the area with fire. It took eight hours for him to die. It was an awful way to go and upset everyone.

On DIS, C Company had some cold mutton and biscuits for breakfast. That's all they had. During the early morning two Jap snipers were firing from Jail Hill and killed one of the sergeants, Arthur Crathern, who shared one of the forward trenches with Roy Wellings. Nobby Hall was also hit. They got him back into Corporal Norman's weapon pit, but the medics couldn't get to him without being hit themselves. He died after a few hours. You couldn't do much about it. You didn't know where the enemy were and just kept your head down. The Japs waited until dusk before launching their infantry attack on DIS, preceded by the usual mortar barrage. The weather was vile. The rain pelted down and made a hell of a racket on the metal roofs of the bashas. Despite this, one ammunition store was ablaze and lit up the surrounding area, so movement was restricted. We didn't see them forming up but as they charged, they used grenade launchers again, showering our positions with high explosives forcing us to keep our heads down as long as possible. They didn't get past the rifle and machine gun fire from four weapon pits some ten yards from the road. Bill Moxworthy was in one, a Corporal and two privates in another and Lance-Corporal Albert Hankinson in another with Privates Lawrence, Goodall and Naylor. Below them were Corporal Webber and his crew. They all had Brens and mowed the Japs down in droves. Despite the vast superior numbers, no one retreated. Men were killed in their trenches rather than falling back. Dennis Cook a Lance-Corporal was in one of C Company's forward positions. The Japs were everywhere. He thought his number was up but was fortunate enough to survive to tell his tale. Many were killed or wounded. We used everything to stop them, rifles, Brens, grenades and bayonets in the close quarter hand to hand fighting on the parapets of trenches. They didn't get past. The Jap 58th Regiment tried to use ladders on the steep, inaccessible slopes to the side of the road. Grenades were used to repel them but they kept trying. As we were forced back, the Japs began to occupy some of our vacant trenches making things very difficult for our lads in the nearby positions. We eventually forced them out but not without further losses. The Japs mounted three separate assaults at the hill, each with over two hundred fresh troops. The Brens got so hot that the barrels had to be repeatedly changed and ammunition used so quickly that the supply to the guns was difficult to maintain. As the Japs charged we fired and they fell like ninepins. Their losses were horrendous but they didn't seem to be bothered, they kept coming and we kept shooting. C Company had many casualties but they held out, the Japs not taking any ground whatsoever. D Company also suffered badly with men being killed and wounded. A mortar killed Corporal Want and 16 Platoon was reduced to three men. The attack lasted for nearly three hours, finishing about 10 pm. An hour later, Naylor heard a jeep and went back to report it. As he came up the hill someone thought he was a Jap and shot him in the leg. They took him back to the ADS. The Japs were so close to our lines that C Company couldn't repair their trenches and any movement was virtually impossible. Eight Brens were arranged in a cross fire and the ammunition supply improved to the forward trenches. No other improvements were possible. This didn't seem to register with the Japs, they moved about freely; so we shot them. Tom Greatley watched in amazement as a Jap officer wandered up the road. He dropped his trousers and squatted down to go to the toilet without any regard as to who could see him. Tom didn't allow him any privacy and shot him. C Company were exhausted through lack of sleep. Losses were high and the defensive perimeter could not be properly manned.

Men tried to collect water during the incessant, pelting rain, using their helmets, dixies or anything else that would do the trick. Any amount collected would help quench what was now a constant thirst but it was never enough. The Japs attacked the Tennis Court at ten in the evening preceded by the usual artillery and mortar bombardment. You couldn't see much from A Company's position because of steep slopes, so we didn't see them form up on the lower terrace. We could hear them though, with their screeching and yelling, so knew they were coming. Contact was made with Major Yeo's 24th Mountain Battery guns outside the perimeter and Victor King's mortars. They let them have it with very accurate fire within twenty yards of A Company's lines. Not one of our lads was hit. Despite this the enemy was still able to initiate an infantry charge and get through to A Company's lines. We couldn't see them coming in the darkness and mist but silhou-

Ted Culmer

ettes and shapes suddenly appeared in front of us. There was no time to pick your target, there were too many. We used grenades and the Brens swept the area. That did the trick. The attack only lasted half an hour but A Company suffered losses and reserves were called in. During the battle A Company's CSM went to collect some grenades from alongside one of the bashas. He heard voices inside and continued with the job in hand until he realised they were Japs. He immediately fetched a section of men and armed with a Tommy gun and grenades cleared the hut, killing those inside. The Japs continued to attack through the night at various positions trying to penetrate A Company's line. It was pitch black and together with the pouring rain and noise of the battle it was impossible for Major Tom Kenyon, in charge of A Company, to know what was going on. The Japs seemed to be everywhere. Sergeant Brooks and his men were under a great deal of pressure from Jap attacks by the Clubhouse. We threw grenade after grenade down the slope onto the enemy on the terrace below and those that made it up were cut down by Bren and rifle fire. Corporal Ted Culmer was there. He had two brothers in the Battalion, Wally and Tom. Wally was also at Kohima. Ted was originally in the Motor Transport section as a dispatch rider. He won the MM (Military Medal) in France. The Germans fired an incendiary bomb into their hut. Before it could go off he picked it up and threw it out saving their lives. Here he manned a Bren, pointing it towards the Jap lines. When the thunder and lightning started so did the Japs. They sent over the mortar barrage followed by the infantry charge at the same time showering the positions with grenades. Culmer emptied magazine after magazine of bullets into them with his private changing them as they ran out. The Japs got to the edge of A Company trenches where they hesitated where to run. Culmer and the others mowed them down until there were none left. The second wave followed shortly after but by this time Yeo's mortars had reduced their numbers. There were still too many. Again Culmer and the others fired. Sergeant Brooks brought him some more ammunition. He was using so much. By now the Bren barrel was too hot. He shouted to his private to change it fearing it would jam, but he'd been wounded in the chest and lay at the bottom of the trench. He had to change it himself hoping that the Japs wouldn't get him during the break in firing. They didn't and he continued replacing the magazines himself until it all went quiet. Despite the enemy pressure all attacks were successfully thwarted and A Company held on.....just. The action of the day caused further losses amongst which were Lance Corporals Sam King and Reg Bowles and Private Reg Cook.

Another attack that night was inflicted on the Assam Rifles' position on IGH Spur. The Japs undertook probing attacks to assess the strength of their defence. The next morning the dead Japs were identified as part of the 138th Regiment of the 31st Japanese Division. We already knew we were up against the 124th Regiment and now, with this evidence, we were aware of the massive number of the enemy, approaching nearly fifteen thousand men. We had at the beginning of the siege only one thousand combatants at most. Things were looking distinctly bad.

CHAPTER 4

In the early light of the 10th April C Company watched in despair as the Japs moved forward into the vacated front line trenches. They moved the bodies of the dead men, theirs and ours, poured petrol over them and set them alight. We watched our dead comrades burn. The stench of burning flesh was terrible and upsetting. It was wet and misty after the storm the previous night and both C and D Companies were desperately short of men. They hadn't been at full strength at the start of the siege. A and B Companies weren't that bad, but were not at full strength. B Company had never replenished its numbers after the barrage by the Tunnels. C Company had now suffered over fifty percent casualties and with the Japs occupying the forward trenches their position was far from secure. Reinforcements were needed urgently. Later that morning Laverty sent reinforcements from HQ Company. C Company were ordered to hold for the rest of the day and withdraw to FSD (Field Supply Depot) that evening. Whilst awaiting the order to withdraw C Company busied themselves by booby-trapping the approaches to DIS and FSD and destroying the plentiful supply of food stocks and stores so that the Japs couldn't use them. Vehicles and equipment were pushed into the nullahs. Tom Greatley a private in C Company punctured the fruit tins so they would go off in the heat, drinking some of the juice to quench his thirst. Tons of tins of bully beef and fruit were destroyed this way. We couldn't take them with us; it wasn't possible, but we had to make sure the Japs couldn't get their hands on them. On one occasion Tom asked a chap in a nearby trench for some food. He obliged and threw a can of Soya link sausages to him and caught him in the face. Tom asked whose side he was on.

We were in a terrible state by now, soaking wet and exhausted from the constant battle conditions and lack of sleep. We stopped washing and shaving days ago and we all sported beards. Our hair was getting longer and we stank. That together with the smell of death and battle was disgusting. The parapet to our trench smelt like a urinal but we were lucky. We could use a redundant shell hole to do our business. They couldn't in the front line. They had to go in the trench and there was not much room to manoeuvre there. Tom Greatley told me that his mate would turn the other way whilst he did 'the necessary' into one of the old SEAC (South East Asia Command) magazines. He would wrap the contents up and throw them as far as he could towards the Jap lines. He didn't know if he hit anyone. He couldn't leave his head up that long but it was a nice thought. Battle fatigue wasn't a problem for the Japs. They sent in fresh troops every time, so it didn't affect them. It was different for us, we couldn't rest. There was the continual threat of snipers and sporadic gunfire. It made food difficult to distribute from the cookhouse. It was almost impossible to get it to the front line; they had to do with bully beef and biscuits. Food wasn't the main concern. It was more important for the men to have effective weapons and water to quench their now desperate thirst. They constantly cleaned their rifles and Bren guns so they wouldn't jam when under attack. More so the Brens; they were such an important weapon. We would've been lost without them and the grenades. This daily regime helped take our minds away from the constant craving for water and keep us alert so we wouldn't drift off to sleep.

Tokyo Rose, the Jap propaganda radio station taunted us, claiming our own army had deserted us and left us to be killed. They tried to get the Garrison to surrender their arms in exchange for good treatment. It all went quiet for a moment. Then the Brens opened up. There was no way we would surrender. We'd heard of the atrocious treatment the Japs gave to those they captured. Surrender was a disgrace to them and they treated their captives with barbaric contempt, often torturing them before wrapping them up with barbed wire and tying them to a tree for bayonet practice. That happened to one of our lads called Sinclair. He was captured at Kohima. Tom Greatley knew him and his mother. When he got back home after the War, he just couldn't tell her the suffering her son went through, it wouldn't have been fair.

About midday Lance-Corporal Hankinson and a section of men were detailed to go forward to a position within ten yards of the Jap lines with orders to hold their positions until C and D Companies withdrew, back to FSD (Field Supply Depot) Ridge. It was a horrible job, suicidal in my mind. They were in a desperate state, exhausted and soaking wet, but they didn't complain. They must have had some bottle. They all deserved medals. They went right into an area where they were surrounded and if the Japs saw them they would have had it. Their action helped give us time to lay booby-traps, destroy food supplies and burn the remaining bashas. They held their position for nearly six hours before they pulled back, virtually crawling all the way. Hankinson was wounded later during the shelling of FSD. Our withdrawal wasn't easy. The Japs on Jail Hill sent over sporadic mortar fire, but really let us have it at dusk. The snipers were always waiting to catch us off guard. Lieutenant Phythian and B Company

Gordon Inglis

officer, Gordon Inglis were hit by snipers. Inglis was detailed to get some ammunition from one of the bashas, but was hit. He died some weeks later in hospital. During the evening C Company withdrew under constant mortaring by the enemy. Easten was shouting orders to Sergeant Boxwell when a mortar shell caught them. It blew Boxwell to bits. Easten was thrown into a trench by the blast, his back dislocated and arm wounded. He was taken to the ADS. Captain Fred Collett took over from Easten. C Company had further casualties. Privates, Stan Weeks, Gerry Bloomfield, Cliff 'Ernie' Foord and John Haslam were killed. C Company was no longer a viable unit because of their losses and joined up with D Company and Tom Coath took command.

A Company weren't in any better condition. If it hadn't been for the effective head cover they would have suffered horrendous casualties and would never been able to hold their line. On several occasions the forward trenches ran out of ammunition. Sergeant Williams repeatedly ferried boxes of grenades to the front line despite the horrendous enemy fire and also helped reorganise the positions. He got the MM (Military Medal) for that. He was very brave. They all were.

Two old experienced men manned a Bren, dug in on the Mound. We didn't know who they were. They weren't West Kents. They were from the odds and sods. They did a brilliant job though. Their accurate fire cut the Japs to pieces as they attacked in wave after wave across the Tennis Court below them. I don't know how many they killed but the Japs lost a massive number of men. The Japs realised what was going on and aimed their fire at them and one of them was killed. The other remained in position and manned the gun himself until a mortar bomb got him as well. Intermittent shellfire rained down on A Company most of the day shaking the bunkers and weapon pits, temporarily blinding and choking the men inside with dust and smoke. Men were killed or badly wounded and most of those that remained were shell-shocked. That was the intensity of the barrages. After each one, bent and splintered weapons were replaced and the defensive positions checked and repaired and the men stood up and prepared for the expected infantry charge. But it didn't come. The line had held firm again. Dennis Wykes, better known to his men as 'Bill,' a corporal in A Company, was in a trench by the Tennis Court with a young Welsh lad called Williams. He was desperate for something to eat. He always was. So much so, that after one of the barrages he decided to run back in an attempt to get some biscuits. He jumped out of his trench and made about ten yards before the next shell exploded. It had hit a tree four feet off the ground and the blast threw him to the floor. He looked up and saw the smoke from the shell and scrambled hell for leather back into his slit trench, tumbling in headfirst. To his horror he saw that the young Welsh lad had been hit in the stomach by a piece of shrapnel. The young lad grabbed Bill's hand and begged him not to let him die. Bill comforted him as best he could and called for the medics and they took him to the ADS. He didn't make it though. To this day Bill doesn't know what made him run from his trench at that particular moment. He would probably have been killed if he hadn't.

The Japs put down over one hundred mortars in ten minutes around BHQ and the ADS that evening. They killed and re-wounded many already injured. The stench was unbearable as men sat in their own excreta and urine. They had no bedpans. Parts of dead bodies were sticking out of their shallow graves. The persistent rain had washed away the cover.

Clouds of flies congregated around the dead and wounded, settling on men's wounds creating further infection. The rain was getting into the shallow trenches of the wounded. They were lying on liquid mud. The numbers of casualties were increasing all the time. The Indians even gave up some of their rations so the wounded could have a little more. In the operating pits, Young and his doctors worked incessantly with hardly any rest. What rest they got was taken fully clothed in what space they could find. Most of the time they snatched an hour or so here and there and it was back to work. They worked in primitive conditions. They'd seen over six hundred cases by the end of the siege. Amputations were done with knives. Their over use made them blunt, more like a hacksaw blade. They must have been under a terrific amount of stress with shells falling all around. They had to treat all types of injury. Men were re-wounded or previous wounds became infected. They never complained. One doctor called Glover was shot on no less than two separate occasions by snipers only to be patched up and carry on. Even the wounded mucked in where they could, helping each other and giving words of comfort to those in a worse condition. Major Shaw who was wounded earlier in the siege was inspirational despite the pain he must have suffered. He was always asking about what was going on at the front. He tried to pass the time by reading Shakespeare while trapped in his trench but couldn't concentrate on it. Padre Randolph lent him a bible. He found that easier and simpler to read.

We realised the situation was becoming dire. Our casualities were mounting, James Bradstreet, a Welsh lad called Dave Bunnell, Ivor Gwilt, Derrick Windle and Cecil Robeson were all dead. Not one of them was older than twenty one. Don Oliver and George Mann, also privates were killed as well. Would it be our turn next? These and other dark thoughts would come and go, especially on long night guard duties. There would be thoughts of food and water, thoughts of home and the probability that we would never see it again. We had that feeling of not being in charge of our lives, like condemned men. We couldn't run away. No one was going to take our place or do our job for us. Fate had decided we were going to fight in this battle and all of us had been picked for this period in time. Every man on this hill had been picked by fate and some, maybe all, would die. I thought a lot about home or going on leave, about eggs and chips, but most of all about water. I was desperate for something to drink. I went across to the cooks and asked for some water. Jack Eves filled my mug but told me not to ask again. The cooks kept us fed, a meal in the morning and another in the evening. The poor sods in the front line had nobody to ask.

I think everyone prayed at some stage. I did. It was all we had left sometimes. Trapped in my trench I would read a strip of paper with prayers and writing from St John, "Let not your heart be troubled neither let it be afraid." I read it over and over again. This piece of paper was given to me in a church canteen in England some eighteen months before although, at the time, it seemed more like a hundred years. Those eighteen months had passed very quickly and only four of them had been in action. It seemed funny that eighteen months of your life could pass so fast, yet seem such a long time ago. It was during this time that a bit of a mystery man appeared around BHQ. He was a lean, clean-cut type of man, English spoken, but with no visible rank and dressed like us in jungle green. I thought he may have been the District Commissioner, Charles Pawsey, or the Garrison Commanding Officer, Colonel Hugh Richards, but never knew for sure. He was a kind chap and moved around the hill lifting our spirits as he moved between our trenches and BHQ. He stopped and talked to us saying that relief would get through and told us not to worry too much. We never knew who he was or where he came from and thought perhaps, he was one of the odds and sods from the early defence units. He seemed without fear of bullets and shells as he strolled along in the open as if defying the enemy. We never saw him again. The funny part about it was that no one ever brought him up in conversation either. But I always would remember this man as he always had a smile and a friendly nod and was one of the few morale boosters for us troops in the trenches.

On the night of the 10th one of the forward A Company positions received a direct hit. Sergeant Bennett immediately led some men forward under heavy enemy fire to replenish the positions and held off the frequent Jap attacks until relieved. The Japs continued to attack during the night of the 10th and 11th concentrating on FSD, to where C Company had fallen back and around the District Commissioner's Bungalow where A Company were. Showers of grenades were launched before their infantry was sent forward yelling and screeching. A Company took the brunt of it but gave nothing away. The attacks were so fierce that one Scottish private picked up three automatic weapons from dead colleagues and emptied each one in turn into the oncoming Japs. There was no time to reload. After that he hurled his grenades before resorting to hand to hand fighting. At dawn the Japs sent over a particularly heavy mortar barrage during which we had further losses and more wounded. Amongst these, Captain Topham was wounded. My trench mate Clayton was his batman and runner and this upset him. He got on well with him. Topham was a nice, kind, happy person who used to come on some of the runs with me. We would often go out with a roll of thin telephone wire and lay new or dummy runs of cable or repair those damaged. Poor Topham was re-wounded at the end of the siege when a shell exploded nearby as they were putting him onto one of the lorries. He died in hospital later.

11th April was a quieter day if you can call it that. The Japs still attacked and sent over their shells, but it wasn't as intense as previously. We were still stuck in our trenches. We couldn't go anywhere. Clayton had Topham's pack and took it to the signals bunker. He was told look after it in our trench until the action was over. That was a pain, as we didn't really have the room. In the pack were several paperback books and I demanded to have one. It would have been great to have something to read to take my mind off the battle, but Ron refused. They were his Officer's property and not his to loan. I felt very angry but he was adamant and would not part with any and so that was that. I was too thirsty to argue and although annoyed, I respected his loyalty. Trapped in our trench, Ron and I would talk about which way would be the best way to escape if it came to every man for himself. We would look at the mountain range and devise a make-believe plan, knowing full well that we would have to fight hand to hand if it came to that. We would also talk of the leave we would get and what we would do when we got to Chowringee in Calcutta. Perhaps we would go to Firpos, a well-known restaurant. Everyone went there. We would order duck with green peas and potatoes, washed down with ice-cold beer. That was our dream. We talked of the many other places we would visit and days and nights out. Maybe we would have a night out to an air-conditioned cinema. But we had to get out of this siege and the odds were distinctly against us. At Kohima, we didn't really have any idea of dates and times. This was judged by the food we received. We got a meal in the morning and a meal at night. Those at the front struggled on bully beef and biscuits. We would talk of home to try and take our minds off the situation we were in, but our thoughts soon turned to water and the chances of getting any from the cooks in the long trench nearby. The cooks allowed us to fill our mugs once more and warned us not to ask again because the water was for cooking food for everyone in HQ. We took the hint and never did but were glad and thankful for our extra ration. They did a cracking job keeping us fed in such conditions. Just because they were cooks, don't think they weren't brave. They were, incredibly so. Colour-Sergeant Jack Eves was seen several times manoeuvring his large six foot four inch frame from trench to trench bringing warm food and tea. He appeared to show little concern about enemy snipers and shellfire. It was actions like his that lifted morale and made us more determined to hold on despite the odds. He didn't only deliver the food. He was in the action too. On

Jack Eves

one occasion he was by the DC's Bungalow and heard noises in one of the bashas nearby. It was some Japs smoking and talking. Jack and another sergeant threw some grenades in and killed them.

Superstition played a great part on some of the men. Corporal Alf Judge had been put in charge of some wounded men and was to help moving them. He was upset because he had lost the lucky teddy bear. His wife Doreen had given it to him when they parted. She had told him that while he had this bear, he would be safe. He felt he was in danger because he had lost it. As he helped the wounded away a Jap shell killed him. I made a mental note not to have any lucky mascots in action should we ever get out of this mess. Others reacted differently and seemed to show little regard for anyone. A rough and ready Scotsman went round collecting gold teeth from dead Japs. No one said anything to him. They just let him get on with it. He would check out the body and simply stamp his heel on the appropriate area to remove the tooth. I don't know what he did with them, but he had a bag full. The local Naga Indians were as bad. They were headhunters prior to the war and delighted in returning back after a sortie with ears of Japanese soldiers.

On FSD, C Company had their first cooked breakfast since they arrived, but not all of them had withdrawn. Due to the battle conditions men had become isolated or had not heard the order. Tom Greatley woke up when he heard talking above the head cover of his weapon pit. The language was Japanese. It was a hell of a shock. He was so scared he couldn't speak. That was just as well. He had to lay low until they moved on. When the coast appeared to be clear he jumped up, picking up his Bren and bandoliers of ammunition and ran for his life towards FSD. He didn't know if he would make it or whether the Japs could see him. He daren't look back and kept going, fearing he would be shot in the back. His helmet fell off as he ran. He didn't bother picking it up. Running as fast as he could he approached a large shell crater. He felt he didn't have time to negotiate clambering in and out of it, so jumped right across it with Bren and all. To this day he doesn't know how he did it; it was a hell of a distance, but he did and made it to the relative safety of his own lines. He didn't know what happened to the others. He didn't see Lockyer and Lewis again. At the same time Roy Wellings was also still on DIS with Corporal Joe Dent, Wellings had acquired a Bren, the gunner Crosbie having been wounded, dying some days later. They too had to bide their time before joining the others.

Three men appeared, came down from the command post and stopped by our trench for a chat and smoke. They were in no hurry to go and do the dangerous job that they had been detailed to do, getting rid of a machine gun post on the road somewhere near the front line. Their talk was light, of other things, perhaps getting some leave in India, but not their thoughts. They wanted their cigarettes to last forever. Their future was uncertain. I felt sad as they left and wished them good luck, feeling thankful that it wasn't us. Some time later, one of them returned, badly wounded, supported by two other soldiers from a forward trench. When asked about the others, he shook his head and tears filled his eyes.

After dark, B Company, led by Major John Winstanley took over A Company's positions around the District Commissioner's Bungalow, with A dropping back to Kuki Piquet. Victor King and the mortar platoon took position to the right by the Club and Mound. Tom Hogg took his platoon to the left with Sergeant Glyn Williams to the centre. Winstanley was a medical student before the war and returned home to become a prominent eye surgeon. He had won a Military Cross in the Arakan. As soon as he and his men had settled in the Japs attacked. Winstanley had heard them forming up and asked for artillery back up. He got it from Hill's 24th Mountain Battery and Victor King's mortars, but some Japs got through only to be met by showers of King's grenades and the now familiar 'Johnny get your gun' sound of the Brens that relentlessly cut them down. A small Scottish private manned one of the Brens with the rest of his section in support. He was a bit of a rough diamond, nothing special, but a decent enough sort. Well, he and his men were terrific and from their forward position controlled the Tennis Court. The enemy cottoned on to this and concentrated their fire on his position, sending showers of grenades towards him. He didn't seem to care and stood up whilst firing the Bren to get a better field of fire. As members of his section were being killed, he relentlessly continued firing, shouting all the time for more ammunition and grenades. Eventually there was only him left, but he carried on loading and firing his gun and throwing grenades. He and his men must have shot hundreds, but they got him in the end. Winstanley found him slumped over his Bren when he returned with some ammunition. The Japs didn't seem to learn from their mistakes. Despite losses they repeated their attacks in the same way. They always did. Twice more they attacked B Company that night and twice more they were repulsed with heavy casualties. The second and third attacks were heavier with the aid of horrendous mortar fire and showers of hand launched grenades. B Company's losses weren't light. The place was saturated with Japs and they now held the area east of the Tennis Court as well as the area around the District Commissioner's Bungalow. We still held the high ground and the positions around the Clubhouse although the Japs managed to get snipers in some trees that overlooked the area. Several of Hogg's 10 Platoon were lost before we discovered from where the Japs were firing. Then some of the lads sorted them out. Due to the lack of tree and leaf cover the Jap snipers were having a field day. They didn't discriminate; they shot anyone who appeared within their sights including the non-combatants and the wounded. It must have been awful for the poor wounded in those shallow slit trenches. There was hardly any cover and chaps would see their comrade next to them shot, not knowing if they would be next; especially those who couldn't help themselves. Winstanley moved Hogg's

Tom Hogg

platoon, or rather the eight men that were left in it, to the Clubhouse. Tom Hogg set up three Bren guns. The Japs attacked both sides but the position was held. One Bren gun crew was lost and Hogg had to man the position himself. In the early hours of the morning, under a full moon, Hogg heard Japs on the Tennis Court. It wasn't the usual screeching and wailing attack. They didn't wear boots, just a type of plimsoll that disguised their advance. About a dozen of them rushed the position with fixed bayonets. One Jap charged at Hogg. Hogg tried to shoot him but couldn't get his shot off in time. The Jap drove his bayonet at him but fortunately for Hogg, it got caught in his belt webbing, hardly injuring him at all. Hogg didn't mess about. He wasn't going to give him a second chance and emptied the twenty-five round magazine into him. The main attack followed with the Japs going through Hogg's positions, but fortunately Winstanley and his men to the rear sorted them out and the position held firm. The next day Hogg was in his position at the corner of the Tennis Court. Lance-Corporal Hill, his only surviving NCO asked if he could go with him should it come to every man for himself. Hogg of course agreed but at the same time a grenade was lobbed into their trench. Hill turned his back on it and was severely wounded. Hogg remained uninjured. It took over a week for Hill to die. There were three survivors of Hogg's 10 Platoon at the end of the siege. Despite this so called 'quieter' day our death toll still rose. Not only from the action of the day but men succumbing to their wounds due to the less than basic medical facilities that prevailed. It wasn't the medics fault. They could only use what they had. Nevertheless, the likeable cockney barrow boy Corporal Bill Moxworthy, another Londoner Fred Gipps and the Welsh lad Will Davies all died. Married men such as Charlie Sims, Sergeant Les Peacock, Privates 'Ginger' Les Fisher, Charlie Trussler and Gwilym Jones would never see their families again.

At first light on the 12th April the Japs attacked two platoons of Rajputs on FSD. They copped a right battering and the Japs had to withdraw leaving thirty of their dead strewn across the hill. Our casualties weren't light. The ADS was past overflowing. Men were moaning in the slit trenches for treatment or something to relieve their pain. The medics were hopelessly short of medical supplies and never seemed to stop to rest. We heard that Sergeant Harry Chartles and Private Eddie 'Tubby' Whittingham were killed. The water situation was becoming desperate and ammunition was running low especially grenades. We would have been in trouble if they'd run out. Some of the men reckoned they were the best weapons at Kohima, especially at night when you couldn't see the enemy to shoot, and they didn't give your position away when used, like the flash or noise from a rifle. Tom Greatly heard that the Japs got hold of some of our grenades but didn't know how to use them. They threw them at our lads with the pins still in. Our chaps obliged by throwing them back with the pins withdrawn.

It was thought that airdrops would do the trick. There wasn't any alternative, there was no other way to get supplies and even airdrops would be difficult in that terrain. We had been pushed back into an area no more than five hundred by five hundred yards, less than that in some places. Every enemy shell seemed to kill or wound someone and that made the situation worse. There were nearly two and a half thousand men in this area and less than one thousand of them were in action, the others being non-combatants or wounded. We were all scared but more so the non-combatants. They weren't used to action. They used to huddle around BHQ not far from my trench. Apparently this was the safest area. I thought to myself if this was the safest place I couldn't imagine what it must have been like in the front line. One thing that did puzzle me about the non-combatants was that although some helped with the wounded or undertook other tasks so that those in action could remain so, many just sat around doing nothing. In fact some refused saying it wasn't their duty. I thought that being in such a position they would have got hold of a weapon and got stuck in rather than waiting to die. Surrender wasn't an option; not after the stories we had heard what the Japs had done to their POWs. I didn't dwell on it all for too long. I had enough to concentrate on keeping myself alive.

That night the Japs were as predictable as ever, letting us have the usual barrages, followed by wild infantry charges or jitter patrols, whereby they would creep up quietly to try to identify our positions to ascertain the best place to attack. During one of the barrages, D Company Sergeant-Major Haines got wounded and was immediately blinded. He didn't go to the ADS though. He refused and ordered a private to lead him around the front line continually barking orders at his men and giving encouragement to build up morale. It worked too. During the actions of the night of the 13th and 14th, Major Peter Franklin led a water party of Indian sepoys to a small spring near B Company's position. About twenty men were there, using small canvas sacks called chagals to collect the water. It took ages to fill them, but over twenty gallons were collected in about five hours and shared between the Companies and the ADS.

Things reached an all time low on the 13th April. The Japs sent over a storm of shells and the ADS suffered two direct hits. It was awful. Over twenty men were killed, including two of the doctors and we couldn't afford to lose them. We didn't have enough medics to start with. Private Paddy Fall was in there being treated for tropical ulcers on his legs. He'd only just had his twenty-fourth birthday the day before. Lance Corporal Albert Harkinson was being treated for wounds to his back. They were killed. Privates Stan Calton, John Brattman and Clement Keating were also lost. Many more of the injured were re-wounded, crying out in pain. A head, limbs and other body parts littered the area. The ADS was completely wrecked and Lieutenant-Colonel John Young, the officer in charge was wounded, but remained on duty and immediately made arrangements for the construction of the new ADS. Barratt's Indians and non-combatants together with some of our lads rebuilt the Dressing Station, which was operational by the afternoon. This time it was more sturdily constructed. It was six feet deep by ten feet long with four-foot trenches to access it. The roof was better too. A mortar hit it shortly afterwards but no real damage was done. Unfortunately, a lot of important medical equipment had been lost and now there wasn't enough medicine or equipment to treat the wounded and men that should have survived were dying because of it. We now knew that however serious the wound, we could not be guaranteed a safe bed. This began to affect the morale of the medics, seeing chaps die after they had their wounds treated because there was insufficient medical care after their operations. It affected everyone really as the medics were a great source of comfort and boost of morale to the men whether they were wounded or not. Fred Worth, a mate of Bill Wykes, was a private in A Company and had been overrun. He got away with it but was shot in the foot when running back. He went to the ADS for treatment but didn't make it. Due to the conditions and lack of proper medical care he caught gangrene and died three days later. It was horrible. You don't expect to die from a foot wound. A Welsh chap called Stenner was luckier. He got lost and had to run back and jumped into the first hole he could. He didn't have time to think. Fortunately it was behind our lines so he was safe. Unfortunately it was the latrine. It wasn't pleasant but better than the alternative.

The water containers in the ADS were punctured during the shelling and the supply lost. The airdrop was now critical. Lives depended on it. If that wasn't bad enough things went from bad to worse. The airdrops were a disaster. You couldn't blame the pilots. It wasn't their fault. The weather was terrible at times and the maps available were only to a very small scale. I don't suppose any better ones existed of that inhospitable terrain. The area we were in was so small it would have been hard to hit if it was flat, let alone amongst the jungle and mountains. A drop zone was agreed and yellow strips were laid out in the shape of the letter 'T'. Indian non-combatants cleared the area under constant sniper fire. Flares were used to guide the first Dakota aircraft in, but the pilot must have passed and dropped the supplies behind the Jap lines. These included a mortar and ammunition that the Japs used against us. The other two planes succeeded with their drops but many of the parachutes landed in the trees and with the Jap snipers about it was a dangerous business retrieving them. You could clearly see the small figures in the aircraft push the cargo out and parachutes blossom, swaying in the wind as they fell. Water was dropped in petrol cans and we watched in despair as the Japs shot holes in them as they hung from the trees. Some of the water cans tore loose from their chutes and crashed into the ground, bursting on impact. The water quickly soaked into the dry ground as thirsty men helplessly looked on. Not all the chutes opened and a couple of Indians were killed when one of the drops landed on them. John Young recovered some of the medical supplies after dark and medicine and painkillers were given to the wounded. This greatly improved the operation of the ADS. However, very little water was recovered and the situation was past desperate. The airdrops continued daily after that.

We had problems on FSD. The Japs were amongst D Company and we couldn't have that. The Assam rifles were sent in to sort it out but couldn't get them all out. They did well but suffered heavy losses and pulled back. Unfortunately the Japs could now fire directly into our trenches. We had to pull back. Since the Japs had taken DIS they could overlook nearly all our positions and with the absence of tree and leaf cover, we were easy pickings. The Rajputs were in a forward position and took a right pasting. Men from A Company relieved them. It was a shame. They had lost their only British officer and this affected these men. Some were in tears. However, their Subedar Sultan Singh, although very upset, rallied them and got them back on track. The rest of A Company came up from Kuki Piquet together with Tom Coath and the remainder of C Company, now reduced to fifteen men. Jap snipers had killed Henry Norton and Lance-Sergeant Morley. A Company saw a suspicious basha on Jail Hill and prepared to mortar it. Before they could, the Japs opened fire and solid shot rained down on us, whistling and ricocheting through the trees, or what was left of them. This was new to us. More Japs were seen and heard casually talking in another basha twenty yards away. Lieutenant Jack Faulkner of A Company was sent to deal with it and went out into the dark armed with a petrol bomb or Molotov Cocktail as we called them. He lit the fuse and threw it against the basha but it didn't go off. He then ran up to the basha and relit the fuse once more and lobbed it through the window opening. This time it did smash and flames immediately filled the basha. The Japs held on as long as they could but had to evacuate. They ran out, some only half dressed, only to be cut down by the platoon Bren which jammed before it could finish the job.

That night the Japs put in desperate attacks on A and D Companies on FSD. The Japs were wearing plimsolls and wrapped their weapons so we couldn't hear them. Lieutenant Doresa ordered his men to hold their fire until the enemy was within fifteen yards; the Bren gunner, Private Peacock, five yards. This was very difficult as the area was saturated with Japs and their shadows were everywhere as they moved amongst the remaining tree and leaf cover. When the order to fire was given the whole platoon joined in and parachute flares lit up the area. A chap in D Company shot three Japs one by one as they jumped into his trench. A and D

FSD Ridge afterwards

Bungalow ruins

Companies lost a considerable number of men, but the Japs losses were heavier still and they were forced to withdraw without any gain. Private Peacock also had a brother in D Company. There was only him in the trench, his trench mate was killed during a mortar barrage. During a qui

Remains of the bungalow from the Tennis Courts

eter moment he dropped off to sleep. It must have been fatigue. When he came round he found he was sharing his trench with a Jap officer, the strange arid sweaty smell gave him away. He couldn't find his rifle and had to fight with his bare hands. After a fierce struggle in the small trench, he broke the Jap's neck and ran him through with his sword to make sure.

The pressure was still intense by the Tennis Court. The bodies of the Jap dead were strewn every-where The stench was awful. B Company's loses were severe. When Sergeant Glyn Williams was wounded in the neck and taken to the ADS, he didn't hang about. Although part paralysed down his one side, he returned to his platoon on the front line. The men were exhausted and this was beginning to take effect. Weapons were jamming on a regular basis. The men were so tired that

Corporal Veall

The Battlefield

The battlefield seen from DIS

The Battlefield

The battlefield

they didn't, or rather couldn't, keep them clean and dry. Private Williams and Corporal Veall were manning a Bren on the mound behind the Club-house when some Japs attacked. The Bren jammed and they bayoneted the corporal. Williams thought he'd had it. He didn't have time to find a weapon. He picked up a shovel and ran at the Japs. He swung it killing

The battlefield

The battlefield

the first Jap and went after the others. To his surprise they ran off. More Japs managed to break through and got into the Clubhouse. This was very dangerous. Victor King attacked them with grenades and that got rid of them. Throughout the night the Japs attacked preceded by showers of hand launched grenades. Bitter battles took place with the West Kents holding their fire until the last possible moment. They inflicted high casualties on the enemy. Then it was down to hand-to-hand fighting and bayonet until the Japs were repulsed again without any gain.

The 13th April was the worst day of the siege so far and became known as the 'Black Thirteenth'. Of the 446 men and officers of the Royal West Kent Regiment that were deployed, 150 were now either dead or wounded. C Company had suffered so many losses that it was no longer a viable unit. Roy Wellings, who had become separated from C Company, remained with Sergeant Brooks and a platoon of A Company until the end of the siege.

On the 14th April, the Assam Rifles relieved B Company by the Tennis Court and Winstanley's men pulled back to IGH Spur. They didn't complete this until almost dark because the enemy snipers were so accurate. We had an airdrop in the morning but one of the planes crashed into Transport Ridge. We didn't know whether any of the airmen survived. We didn't like to think about it. It might have been better if they were killed than to fall into the hands of the Japs. During the rest of the day the Japs peppered the Garrison with mortar fire and high explosive rounds. Some of the wounded had recovered enough to return to their units, making room in the ADS for the less fortunate. Mind you, it wasn't safe in the ADS. Jap shells were always falling around it.

Corporal Arthur Hay was a stretcher bearer and was always in the thick of it. He won the Military Medal in the Arakan for tending the wounded under heavy fire. It was the same at Kohima. He couldn't guarantee that he would get back when called upon to treat the wounded. One night Privates Wheeler and Guilford went out with a stretcher to bring someone in. They didn't return and after ten minutes, Corporal Hay went out to see what was going on. He was coming down with malaria but had to go. There was nobody else. As he reached the forward dugouts he found the stretcher. Guilford was dead. He didn't know what had happened to Wheeler. He went back to his dug out and the malaria finally took its toll. The next thing he remembers is two soldiers grabbing him by the arms, and carrying him off the hill when we were relieved.

A forward patrol spotted four Japs chatting in a bunker on FSD. The Japs saw them too and beckoned them to come over. They didn't know if they were going to surrender or trying to be friendly. Anyway they couldn't take the chance, not with the Japs. The patrol leader went back to his Commanding Officer for orders. They returned with a Bren and a section of men and shot them. It was misty that morning and at about midday the

Japs laid down some smoke and attacked some positions occupied by odds and sods brought in to replace some of our casualties. Nearly forty of them attacked with gelignite and grenades as they tried to blow up our positions. Our men had to retreat up the hill as the Japs moved forward. However, the flanking troops peppered the area with mortars and small arms fire halting the enemy advance and killing many of them as the Japs withdrew. Around ten in the evening the Japs tried to infiltrate through A Company's positions on FSD. We couldn't see them properly. They were just shapes dodging amongst the trees. Some Japs got into one of the bashas. We couldn't let them stay there as they could overlook our positions. We had a hell of a game getting them out. Bullets and grenades weren't working, nor did the Molotov Cocktails. Jack Faulkner using petrol followed by a grenade did the trick, setting the basha alight. The Japs ran out and down the hill into the waiting Bren. Again the fatigue of battle showed as the gun jammed and most of the enemy escaped.

Apart from us at Kohima there were hundreds of multi racial group of people. Many did not have English steel helmets and some had little or no full British uniforms; most had oriental faces. So it was hard to say if someone unwashed, dressed in this or that was on our side or were the enemy. Many were unable to speak English and of those that could, it was rather hit and miss. About three in the morning, three men that I thought were non-combatants appeared. Somehow they had got through our front line positions and now were standing several yards away from me. I ordered them to halt. None of them reached for any weapons. I had my rifle levelled at them. They huddled together. They had no means of identification and so I was uncertain of what to do. Should I blast them away only to find out later I had killed or wounded three, perhaps unarmed, innocent local tribesman, causing the already exhausted troops to stand to, or should I let them pass. Also, what if the people in the front positions heard someone attacking BHQ. What would they do? Perhaps there might be other hidden enemy troops waiting for these three fall guys to take the fire, identifying our positions, so they could attack in force. I was confused and hesitated, but eventually waved them through. They moved on huddled together, with their frightened strained faces looking back as they continued up to the top of the hill, on to the track and out of sight. As I had not received a password from them, I should have shot them. I had learnt that lesson days before while on night guard. I'd heard action down by the Tennis Court in front of us, shouting and fighting. It appeared that the

Japs had broken through and were making their way up and through to BHQ. I immediately grabbed one of my grenades and pulled the pin getting ready to throw it at the oncoming enemy. But they didn't come and I waited several minutes and realised that they had been held. So there I was, standing with this grenade ready to throw, the pin released and discarded on the ground somewhere. Of course, to throw the grenade would be wasting valuable ammunition and would also draw attention to our position. Therefore, we had to look for the lost pin. I held the grenade in one hand and Clayton and I searched the bottom of the trench for the it. After a few nerve-racking minutes, although it seemed an age, Clayton found it. He gave it me and I pushed it back into the grenade. Then I placed the grenade on the parapet in case of further attack and eventually drifted off to sleep. As dawn approached I awoke to see the grenade lying on the edge of the trench with its sprung arm straining to release itself. The split pin had been incorrectly housed with only half of the pin stem being in the correct position, the other half bent out of shape. I immediately woke Clayton up and went across and withdrew the pin. Whilst holding the grenade handle steady, straightened the pin with my teeth and made it safe and put it back into my pack.

Lieutenant Johnson led a patrol of 4/7th Rajputs in. They managed to get through to us from the 161 Brigade that were battling through the Jap roadblocks to relieve us. God knows how they got through in one piece, the area was infested with Japs, but they did. Our Commanding Officer, Lieutenant-Colonel Laverty told him that men's spirits were all right but we were exhausted and there weren't enough of us to hold on much longer. He added that unless help came within forty-eight hours Kohima would fall. Johnson and his Rajputs left and took the message back to their HQ.

On this day, Colonel Hugh Richards, the Garrison Commander, gave an 'Order of the Day'. It read:

'I wish to acknowledge with pride the magnificent effort which has been made by all officers, NCOs and men and followers (non-combatants) of this Garrison in the successful defence of Kohima.

By your efforts you have prevented the Japanese from attaining this objective. All attempts to overrun the Garrison have been frustrated by your determination and devotion to duty. Your efforts have been in accordance with the highest traditions of British arms.

It seems clear that the enemy has been forced to draw off to meet the threat of the incoming relief force and this in itself has provided us with a measure of relief. His action is now directed to contain us by harassing fire, while he seeks to occupy odd posts under cover of that fire.
The relief force is on its way and all that is necessary for the Garrison now is to stand firm, hold its fire and beat off any attempt to infiltrate among us.

By your acts you have shown what you can do. Stand firm; deny him every inch of ground.

I deplore the sufferings of the wounded: every effort is being made to alleviate them at the first opportunity.

Put you trust in God and continue to hit the enemy hard wherever he may show himself. If you do that, his defeat is sure.

I congratulate you on your magnificent effort and am confident that it will be sustained.'

Hugh Richards, Colonel
Commander Kohima Garrison
14 April 1944.

That order was typed out and handed round the troops under fire. It gave us a huge lift and determination to think we might just get out of this alive. But there was still plenty to do. Apart from those wounded we lost fourteen men that day. The worst death toll yet. Three of the Williams' were killed or succumbed to their wounds. Some of the other Welsh lads, Corporal Len Rees, Privates Steve Roberts and Ken Davies were also lost. Amongst the others that had died or were killed were Corporals Eddie Hatton and George Fidler and Privates George Baker, Charlie Gray, Percy Hughes, Don Mancey and Russell Gartrell as well as one of the Collins brothers, Len.

15th April was a regular day; the enemy sticking rigidly to its methods, letting us have the usual artillery and mortar barrages. The heaviest concentrated on FSD, inflicting more casualties on A and C Companies. John Hazell was killed. He was one of the cockneys, married as well. We were told that relief was on its way but didn't take that much notice. That was old news that never seemed to materialise. We hoped it would before it was too late. Apparently, Laverty was told that relief would come the next day and made arrangements for some of the wounded to be evacuated. I never heard anything. It was just as well because it didn't come. We were stuck in our trench by BHQ. We couldn't go anywhere, not with the snipers about. We sat and talked, cleaned our weapons or tried to grab some rest. A flurry of shells finished our conversation and we threw ourselves flat to the floor of the trench. Some appeared to be duds as they whistled down and didn't explode. Later we were told that the shells we thought were duds were armour piercing shells. Some went through the walls of the trenches, killing the men inside. I found one near our trench on my way to our shell hole toilet.

That night I was detailed to water party duty, collecting water from a nearby supply point behind our position. I don't know where it was exactly but I knew it was behind enemy lines. A water supply pipe by the roadway was tapped under the hours of darkness with each of the men taking turns. It was my turn to collect the water for the runners. I moved with the runners' water bottles to join the other shadowy figures of the water party threading their way through the crawl trenches by the ADS, filled with wounded men. It was a pitiful sight and the stench of death and excreta was overpowering. We tried to give words of comfort and support but there was little we could do. I don't know how they coped. We moved down until we joined the others in the main party, each waiting in turn to collect water. Soon it was my turn and I moved down on to the road. The NCO held the pipe while another man took my bottles and filled them. A Bren gunner lay flat behind his gun a couple of yards away, the barrel pointing along the empty road towards the enemy. It seemed to take forever before the bottles were filled and handed back to me. This was a very tense time, four of us alone on the road under the noses of the Japs but it was the only way to replenish our water supply. We had no choice. With the water bottles filled, I quickly climbed up the hillside and rejoined the returning party. This detail would continue throughout the night and the pipe would be reconnected so that the supply point was kept secret from any passing Jap patrols the following day. This operation was done nightly and others would have to take their turn in the days to come. I was only ever ordered to go once and it was scary. I filled my bottles and left. The NCO and Bren gunner were there a lot longer. I don't know if they were relieved but in any event they were exceptionally brave. If anyone deserved a medal at Kohima they did.

That night the Japs sent over their usual barrage. It was repetitive and worked its way up Summerhouse Hill towards our position. Earlier in the siege we got down to the bottom of the trench straight away until the barrage was over. As we got used to it we would watch the shells explode. It wasn't that we weren't scared. We were, but we were hardened now and sick of being stuck at the bottom of a hole. We watched as the Japs dropped mortars on those in front of us. When they got to a certain point we knew it would be our turn next and got down to the bottom of the trench. The first mortar bomb would explode about twenty-five yards or so in front of us with a further six bombs slowly working their way up the slope towards our trench. They always came in sevens. We would count the explosions whilst laying low at the bottom of our trench and after the seventh explosion, jump up with our rifles cocked and bayonets fixed, ready for any attack by Japs that may have broken through the forward positions. We had done this for the last few weeks. Fortunately, in our case, the immediate frontline had always held and the enemy never came. We were lucky though as, just forward of our position, troops were involved in hand to hand fighting with the on rushing Japanese. We could hear them after each barrage, the screaming and shouting of hundreds of Japs as they psyched themselves up for the forthcoming charge, followed by the shouting and screaming of hand to hand combat. It was horrifying, as we never knew whether or not it would be our turn next. After the seventh mortar bomb exploded at the end of each barrage I would tense up waiting to see if any Japs had broken through, followed by the huge relief that our lads had held them off. It was an awful feeling that I experienced every day at dawn and dusk. This particular evening number four mortar exploded on the rear of our trench. Clayton and I lay on the floor at bottom of the trench and had to wait for three more mortar bombs to come and couldn't move until these had all exploded. A thick green smoke filled our trench almost choking us. The explosion blew dirt, pebbles and earth into the trench and on to our packs. A piece of shrapnel ripped open my pack and put a hole through my 1944 diary. Another piece had cut through a bandolier of bullets, neatly slicing through a clip of ten 303s. How they never went off I don't know, but we just counted our blessings that we were still alive. Clayton's blanket disappeared, presumably blasted elsewhere on the hill. We couldn't look for it anyway. For some reason Clayton left his water bottle on the parapet of the trench. It was full of holes, leaving us with one water bottle to share between us. I wasn't pleased about that at all as water was so scarce. We made sure we kept that at the bottom of the trench after that. Suddenly, the man in the next trench, a runner called Williams, panicked and started to get out of his trench to run. I don't know why. There was nowhere to go. Perhaps he thought he would run to the more relative safety of the larger signals bunker but there were three more mortars to come. He must have known that. The poor sod was blown straight back in as number five mortar bomb exploded in front of him. We immediately called for the stretcher-bearers, but they couldn't get him out; the trench was too narrow, so they had to leave him. It was awful for the poor chap. We couldn't risk tending to him for fear of being targeted ourselves so he was left there until the next day when things had quietened down. Then, the medics came to take him to the ADS. When they got there we had to thread a blanket around him, so that he could be lifted out in a sling-like fashion. Although badly injured he was well aware of what was happening and we carried him back to the ADS. Unfortunately, when we got him to sickbay his injuries were so severe that he died three days later. He was married with kids and a good soldier too. He'd served in the Middle East, seeing more action than most. He was a caring sort of chap. It was him that helped a shell-shocked runner that came out of a barrage by the Tunnels. The man didn't know where he was. Fortunately, Williams grabbed him and helped sort him out. He also helped out with the wounded and would often take time out to talk to them as they were carried down. I just think it got to him in the end.

As I looked out of my trench on the 16th April I noticed the remnants of the parachutes from previous airdrops were drooped everywhere over the remaining trees. The ground was now virtually bare, all the leaf and tree cover gone. The day was quieter than usual. Of course we got the usual barrages and they carried out some probing attacks to try and find weak spots. We had more airdrops and these were more successful than earlier ones, with most being recovered by our troops. That evening a Supply Officer slipped us a bottle of rum as he passed and we all had a good drink. I began to feel really merry and started singing aloud, 'Onward Christian Soldiers'. Soon the others joined in and it seemed the whole hill was singing. The Officers let us continue for a while but eventually the order came to be quiet. I don't know what the Japs made of it, but we give little thought to that. Mind you the next barrage seemed heavier. We peered over our trench and watched the first shells and mortar bombs exploding on our forward positions, gradually creeping up towards where we were and beyond. We counted the mortars as they came towards our position. The strain of war was now beginning to tell as, during and after each barrage, you would hear the groans and moans of those that had been wounded. But we were unable to help because if anyone tried to leave their trench they found themselves a victim of mortar or sniper fire. It was an awful mess.

Earlier that day the Japs had positioned a machine gun among some tree cover to the rear of Keene's Bungalow or what remained of it. It was causing a lot of problems to the Assam troops. They tried to knock it out with a mortar but that didn't work. In the end, as it got dark, four men were detailed to attack it led by a local Naga called Angami. They left their trenches and formed up on the terrace above the Tennis Court and made a charge towards the machine gun some forty yards down the hill. Each man held a grenade from which the release pin was removed ready to throw. A Bren gave covering fire from the left. As they ran another Bren opened up from the Clubhouse. The Clubhouse was virtually wrecked and the Bren gunner Sepoy Wellington Massar fired the weapon from the top of the billiard table to get a better field of fire but this was in full view of the enemy. Angami and his men completely wiped out the machine gun post but their action alerted the surrounding Japs Companies who opened fire immediately but Angami and his men managed to get back safely. Unfortunately, Wellington Massar got hit whilst covering their return. However, despite his injuries, he manned the Bren until they got back. He died later in hospital. That day we were told that if we hung on for two more days reinforcements would arrive and we would make history.

We held on for four!

That night was dark and misty. It rained later. The Japs repeatedly attacked the area around the District Commissioner's Bungalow, now not much more than a pile of rubble, but were beaten back every time. In the early hours of the next morning, the 17th April, they attacked FSD pushing A and C Companies back towards the top of the hill. A mixed group of

Assam Rifles and the Assam Regiment relieved A and C and managed to retake some of the positions lost, but the Japs were still too far advanced for comfort. A and C pulled back to the southern slopes of Summerhouse Hill, a former rest area, but now under constant fire. The whole area was a target and there was nowhere free from the Jap shells. My company had also suffered terrible losses and my last run to them was to a young Officer in a weapon pit with perhaps four or five men in it. The area was covered with trees and vegetation at the beginning of the siege, but now the landscape was barren. There was nothing left. When I arrived on FSD I stopped but couldn't see where anybody was. Suddenly, a corrugated sheet of metal that covered the weapon pit at ground level moved and the officer asked what I wanted. I gave him the message which he took with his heavily bandaged wrist covering a wound of some kind. I asked if there were any snipers about and he pointed to the bullet ridden metal dixies, saying that if there was, I was likely know about it fairly quickly. I didn't need any further reminder and left straight away. On my way back it dawned on me that if I had not been transferred from C Company Runner to BHQ Runner, I could have been in that weapon pit, where only a handful of men remained. I think the A Company runner had it worst. One day, towards the end of the siege, he had to go down to the Tennis Court and it was obvious he didn't fancy it. None of us would have, not amongst that lot, but he had to go. He didn't come back. I don't know what happened to him.

Bill Cordwell was desperate for a drink and that night made his way on his own to a water point. It was a stream, no more than a trickle really. He leant over and hung his head down to quench his thirst. After a few moments he lifted his head and glanced downstream. A Jap was doing exactly the same. They were both looking at each other in complete surprise. I don't know if they had any weapons with them. He never said what happened, but he came back. He did say once that he was close to some Jap positions and both sides had mortars but didn't use them so not to provoke retaliation. Mind you that didn't last long and then all hell let loose.

Ivan Daunt, Bernard 'Bomber' Brown, Fred Clinch and others were detailed to a water party. The water point was ten minutes away by the main road. They had to crawl to the source itself because of the fixed line machine gun the Japs had set up. They couldn't see them getting the water but fired every now and then on the off chance of catching someone. Bomber Brown collected the water bottles but in his rush he didn't keep down and two bullets from the Jap machine gun caught him in the backside. It was only a flesh wound. The bullets didn't hit a bone but he had to go to the ADS. Alec (Scoffer) Longley and Dick Hook looked after him at base while the water party completed their task. Bob Clinch arranged for him to be taken to the ADS. Bob and Fred Clinch weren't the only brothers in the battalion. In fact there were several. The Collins's were twins. They both got killed.

Every morning and evening the Japs sent over their barrages as regular as clockwork. It is impossible to describe the strain we suffered. I can only liken it to being put into a firing squad and being reprieved each time. This happened twice a day, every day. The battle still raged and we watched as allied planes swooped down through the smoke and attacked the Japs, but they still kept coming, steadily pushing us back with their barrages and infantry attacks, accepting their massive losses for the small amount of ground gained. I didn't do any more runs. There was no need. The Japs had overrun our positions on the ridges all around. I spent most of the day in the trench straining my eyes into the distant roads and mountains looking for that enemy machine gun that had pinned us down or for a sniper. Some light relief would come as a pair of our fighters strafed the Jap positions in the hills above us with cannon fire and tiny flashes of fire shot up in lines across the hillside. That night the Supply Officer gave us some cigarettes and cigars. Three Ghurkhas had dug in a few yards away, their unit lost in some counter attack, they were now helping in defence around BHQ. Their faces showed the signs of close quarter fighting, being pot-marked with small red cuts and scabs. We gave them the cigars. They would have preferred the cigarettes but we kept them for ourselves.

That evening the Japs really let us have it. They attacked the area around the Tennis Court continuously but the disciplined group of Assam Rifles and Regiment fought them off. The barrage on FSD went on for almost five hours and Summerhouse Hill where I was, copped a right pasting. We knew help was near. Some Punjabi troops were seen about half a mile to the west, working their way towards us. We were all totally exhausted by now. We hadn't had a proper wash or sleep for over two weeks and were bleary eyed and wore scruffy beards. Some men were suffering from dizziness and the shakes, they were that fatigued. We didn't know if we could carry on and hold out until help arrived, but we couldn't give up. We all knew that wasn't the answer. We had to dig deep . Even in these dire circumstances, there was always one or two that would crack a joke or say something funny to lift morale. Unfortunately, the Japs had more luck that night and their persistence paid off with them taking FSD and advancing further to also claim Kuki Piquet. They followed up their barrage with showers of grenades and an infantry attack with phosphorous bombs. These bombs lit up the whole area and were blinding. They set some of the remaining bashas alight. You could hardly see. You couldn't tell friend from foe, not until you were right next to them. Then it was too late and hand-to-hand combat took place. Tom Greatley always thought the Japs took some sort of drug as they seemed to charge without any fear of being killed. He was convinced when during one charge a big Jap led the way and set off a phosphorus bomb and held it to his chest, laughing as he burnt to death. He couldn't see the reason for that. Roy Wellings also thought the Japs may have been taking something and several times noticed that the dead had carried tiny wooden containers with a cork in the top. It may have been ceremonial. He never did find out.

Later, C Company withdrew to Summerhouse Hill. Mortar man Victor King had his jaw shattered by a shell splinter during the last attack on Kuki Piquet but refused to go to the ADS and remained to help his men, holding his jaw together with his hand. Blood was pouring from the wound. Eventually he was persuaded to get treatment only to be blown unconscious by a shell blast whilst standing by the ADS. D Company commander was injured and the blinded Sergeant-Major Haines gave a great deal of encouragement as he was led amongst the men before the enemy eventually killed him. We were pushed back into an area of about three hundred and fifty by three hundred and fifty yards. The front line was so thin due to losses that if the Japs made a concerted effort they would surely break through and that would be it. Roy Wellings was alone in his trench when a Jap fell in. Fortunately he was already dead. Roy didn't know where he came from or who'd shot him. He didn't take any chances and shot him again just to make sure. He had to wait a few hours until it got dark before he could get him out and roll him down the slope. Needless to say he didn't enjoy the company that day.

We could hear the sound of our guns belonging to the second British Division getting nearer. They had started to shell the Jap lines. We all hoped that this would weaken their positions and allow reinforcements to get through to us in time. We were told to keep well down as our own artillery was now massing on the outside of Kohima and would be putting down an extremely heavy barrage onto the Japanese forward positions just a few yards in front of our own trenches. It was a heavy barrage indeed and it was just as well that we kept right down, for as the shells landed bits of shrapnel flew all around, but we were unharmed and glad to see the Japs had got a taste of their own medicine. By now our artillery was bombarding the Japanese positions on the hillsides and the enemy forward positions relentlessly and our reinforcements were getting nearer every day. But the pressure on us troops was immense and although our losses were nothing like those of the enemy, simple arithmetic showed that it must only be a matter of time before we would be overwhelmed, but for some reason they never attacked again that night and so the line was held.

It was now the 18th April 1944. The morning was cold, damp and misty. The situation was touch and go. A, C and D Companies; had withdrawn to the southern slopes of Summerhouse Hill. Sergeant Bill Millichap was killed as they did so. Kentish Lance-Corporal Arthur Hawker was also lost. HQ Company was around the command post area and B Company on Hospital Ridge. We'd lost a lot of men the previous night, but our reinforcements were finally coming. The Punjabis were clearly visible on Piquet Hill and eventually tanks cleared the way through with infantry support to IGH Spur. The Dimapur to Imphal Road was open again. However, the Japs were only one hundred yards from the ADS and the shelling continued, each one claiming further casualties. Ambulances got in and some of the walking wounded and non-combatants walked down the road to try to leave but the Japs saw them and sent a barrage of shells over wounding and killing some. The Japs also had a machine gun mounted on a nearby hillside and a number of snipers round and about. These continued to hinder the evacuation and this led to further casualties. It was felt that if the Japs put in another heavy attack they would get through. I kept my magazine full with ten bullets and my bayonet fixed in readiness for the attack that surely must come. I also kept one bullet up the spout in case it came to hand-to-hand fighting. I'd heard that some men had got their bayonets jammed in the enemy and couldn't free them. I wasn't going to stand for that. I would free it by blasting them off with a bullet.

There was no concerted attacks during the night of the 18/19th until about 4.30 am. Then the Japs attacked from the south taking on an Assam Regiment that was forced to withdraw through A Company's positions. The enemy took advantage of this and occupied positions only five yards in front of A Company. Then the Japs attacked once more and managed to get amongst A Company positions and were now only forty yards from BHQ. Fortunately, A Company were supported by the 1st Punjabis and managed to recapture the area killing nearly twenty of the enemy. A company of Punjabis were also attacked by the District Commissioner's Bungalow and suffered heavy losses. Despite this they held firm, seeing off every Jap attack.

19th April brought more airdrops which were very successful considering the restricted area to aim at. There were casualties from the falling supplies due to the concentration of men and wounded. Those two days to make history had now passed and still no reinforcements had arrived but we fought on. There was no other way. We knew if the 2nd Division didn't get a firm hold that day it would be all over for us. They did. They sent barrage after barrage into the Jap positions. The guns were positioned behind each other on the road outside because of the steep slopes and were meticulously guided to their targets by the ever-present Yeo. Twenty-five pound shells ripped into the enemy positions. Hurribombers relentlessly deposited their bombs slowing the enemy advance. Barrett's Indians and non-combatants continued their magnificent job by ferrying the wounded down to the waiting ambulances and trucks under the constant threat of mortar and sniper fire. Many of the wounded were killed or re-wounded and the great majority of the loading party became casualties. That night we prepared for the worst but the Japs attacks didn't have the usual ferocity. We were grateful for that because our defences were so thin that any attack of substance would have succeeded. The command bunker itself was severely damaged through the constant shelling. Ivan Daunt and the other pioneers had a hell of a job keeping it repaired. But the infantry attack didn't come. Snipers were still active though and unfortunately Captains Harry Smith and Tom Coath were wounded in the actions that did take place. Harry Smith was by the Garrison Command Post when some shrapnel caught him beneath his eye. Bill Wykes was in a forward bunker by the District Commissioner's Bungalow with head cover and a slit in the front for fire and observation. He peered over the top to see what was going on. He heard a swish and a bullet smacked into the rear of the bunker. A Jap sniper must have seen his face. Thank God his aim wasn't that good. He didn't let that happen again. Brummie born Harry Hopkins wasn't so lucky. He was killed.

The men of the First Battalion of the Royal Berkshire Regiment were first in to relieve us and did so on the 20th April 1944. They couldn't believe what they saw. Many of them were retching as they approached our positions. The rancid smell of death and excreta greeted them together with the awful sights of death and carnage. We gave what advice we could. We had to. We couldn't let them face that lot without telling them what to expect. They were better equipped. They had new, more modern weapons, rather than the old Lee Enfield rifles with long bayonets that we had. Some had flamethrowers. I moved out with Ron Clayton and the other runners (that had been left to join the remainder of the BHQ and HQ) and the rest of the battalion rifle companies, plus the walking wounded. Ivan Daunt left his weapon pit, his mates Horace Collins and one of the Browns still in there. Horace was dead. They hadn't had a chance to bury him. Bernard Brown was wounded. Horace and Bernard were packing up, getting ready to move out. Horace was out of his trench when a Jap sniper got him. Bernard Brown heard Horace cry out and looked over the parapet of the trench to see what was happening when the same sniper caught him in the left shoulder. His mates dressed his wound and took him to the ADS. Horace's brother Len was killed a few days earlier. He didn't know about it. We were going to tell him when we'd got out. That wasn't easy either. The Japs continued to shell and snipe us as we left, taking further casualties. Les Rose, a Corporal was also killed before we left. Even the wounded weren't spared and some were killed or rewounded as they were put onto the waiting lorries. Private Walter Forsyth died a couple of days after being taken out.

As we moved down, I noticed that the whole area was virtually barren, the trees and vegetation had been blasted away and just jagged spikes remained of the previous tree cover. Parachutes hung on some of those trees that were left from previous airdrops their contents long gone. We continued down to a sheltered gully with its cliff like sides finding dead Japs here and there. An upper part of a dead Jap was propped up against the bank in part of the gully; just the chest, shoulders and head, his lower torso and legs were completely missing. The debris of war was everywhere; Jap bodies, helmets, rubbish, everything. We were the lucky ones, thousands weren't. Sherman tanks pointed their guns at the Jap positions protecting the withdrawal and those troops moving up to take over our positions. The trucks waited on the road. Their clean-shaven drivers and others looked on in amazement as they helped us on. We didn't realise we were heroes but the clean-shaven drivers and others did. They clapped and cheered us as we came down. 'Shabash, Royal West Kents!' the Indians shouted.

Kohima aftermath

Lorries on the Imphal Road

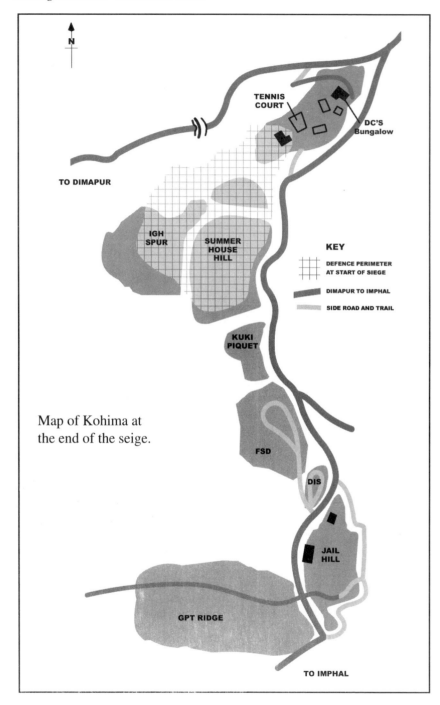

Map of Kohima at the end of the seige.

Troops after Kohima

*Laverty receiving the DSO
from Mountbatten*

109

Everyone looked at us in surprise, not expecting heroes to look unshaven, dirty with long hair, stinking from the inability to wash and red eyed from lack of sleep. We were lost in our own thoughts and took no notice. We just settled down in the trucks and fell asleep with fatigue straight away as the trucks trundled down the mountain road towards Dimapur. A few miles down the road we were woken up for a meal and some tea, then off again, back to the base near Dimapur for a longer rest. We slept through the next twenty-four hours, missing meals, despite being called and woken up for them. Several razor blades were needed to cut off our beards which had grown during the siege. We cleaned ourselves up. Two lorries turned up with big copper tanks. They parked up and set up showers between them. They were hot too. I don't know where they got the hot water. I didn't care either. Actually they were too hot but it didn't matter, we felt a lot better for it. Some of the men had to shave their bodies because of lice and insects. We were all sprayed with some type of DDT or disinfectant. Twenty-four hours later we were called into a large marquee. The CO told us what we had achieved in buying time for others to smash the Japanese advance on India. He told us he had been awarded the DSO, but it was for all of us, not just him. In a strange way I missed the bombardment.

The sixteen day siege cost us dearly. Seventy eight men killed and nearly two hundred wounded.

CHAPTER 6

We were still in a rest area when our new NCO detailed me and some others to watch out for enemy aircraft in case of an air raid. He gave me a whistle to blow should I spot any. We were allowed to wander around while on duty doing our own thing and had not seen any enemy aircraft for weeks. Then one day, I spotted a group of aircraft in steady formation over Kohima. Suddenly there was a loud explosion as bombs were dropped. I blew my whistle and raced to my trench. The NCO appeared at my side saying, "Bit late with that whistle weren't you, Street."

"I thought they were ours," I replied as we dived into our trench.

Jap fighters started to strafe the road below and as one flew over our heads I slammed a couple of shots into him quickly aiming at his wings but he had gone in seconds. Another circled round climbing higher to clear the trees. I sent more shots into his fuselage but the plane soon disappeared from view. All was then quiet, the tank guns had stopped, the rifle fire had stopped but a minute or two later I spotted what I thought was another Jap plane flying on the course set by those we had just fired at and missed. It seemed slower as if searching for a target, coming in from behind a group of trees. I quickly decided to take a really good aim at this one, put my hand up and took the range and fired straight into the cockpit. To my horror I saw the RAF markings on the fighter which started to waggle his wings to signal that he was friendly. But it was too late. All the other rifles in the valley opened up. However, the tanks did not fire nor did our automatic weapons as they recognised him immediately. Fortunately he flew off to safety. We didn't see any more planes after that.

After Kohima we had a new NCO, a hard but fair man. His method of 'on parade, on parade' and 'off parade, off parade,' worked well with the men. He was a loyal man to his troops and once, when drinking in a bar with some of them on leave, knocked a chap spark out, for criticising his 'West Kents.'

It was May 1944 when we moved back towards Kohima and the monsoon had started again. The Japs were retreating, with many trapped, trying to break out back to their own lines. Others had fled into the hills. Although in a rest area, we were just behind the front line and could hear the action in the distance. Our chaps hit a Jap ammunition dump and we were treated to a spectacular 'firework' display, with explosions. The fires burned continuously for three days and nights.

We moved round the back roads high above Kohima towards the Jessami track, a route that started by the cemetery with English style gravestones and ran through thickly wooded and jungle ridden mountain sides to link Kohima with the Imphal Road. We passed a burnt out British tank with a shell hole in the back of its turret. Later we moved over an old Jap position and there were the bodies of about a thirty British and Indians on the slopes, now just uniforms and bones.

On the top of a ridge was a row of blown out Jap bunkers with their contents looking like something out of a horror film. Dead Jap skulls grinned from under their helmets as their bodies sprawled on the bottom of their blown out positions. We went by, happy that those chaps on the slopes had not died in vain. We passed through some of the Worcestershire Regiment positions and I saw some old friends from my Norton Barracks days. One of them was Private Hill. I stopped and had a rest and natter about old times. During our chat he dropped mortar bombs down the barrel of his weapon and fired them at the enemy. Without breaking sentence, he would simply adjust the sight and continue firing as we talked. We stayed the night near there and at first light we moved down towards the Jessami track.

We moved in single file down the track. We were at the head of the column with the other members of signals platoon and the CO. Mules were the main, and sometimes the only, form of transport. They carried food, provisions and equipment on the mountain tracks. These tracks were only wide enough to let others pass by with very little room to spare. We felt sorry for the mules with their heavy loads. There was a love-hate relationship with them and their Muleteers. Sometimes their loud braying would give away our position. The Muleteers themselves would fuss these animals and scratch around for extra food or titbits to feed them, treating them as pets. They got really close to them, so much so, I once remember seeing a Muleteer crying, poor chap, because one of his mules had fallen over the edge of track and down the mountainside, dragging the two others with it.

After a few days we joined up with one of the SAS type units. They were fresh faced young lads that had not been in the jungle long but they had cleared that part of the Jessami track of Japs. One early misty morning at first light we overran a Japanese camp. The enemy had left in a hurry leaving everything as it was. They couldn't have been gone long. A billy-can of water was still boiling on the fire. Rifles were stacked neatly in threes and uniforms still hung on bushes. I kicked the tin into the fire and we took the bolts out of the rifles and threw them down the jungle covered hillside. We went through the pockets of the uniforms for information but most were empty.

A dead Jap was on a stretcher and I walked past leaving him alone, kicking a blood stained white rag as I went by. My friend behind picked it up and to my disappointment shook it out to find it was a large Japanese battle flag with a tiger on it, a fine souvenir, nice and light and easy to carry. We continued to search the camp but found nothing and started to go back. That so-called dead Jap had got up and gone. He was lying dogo and waited for the opportunity to leave. We wouldn't be so foolhardy next time.

Japanese units were holding the mountain side positions at the edge of the road going back to Kohima and, as we moved down, we got a view of the heavy guns firing up at the roadside enemy positions. A few hours later, we had heard Vickers heavy machine guns firing. It was the 6th June 1944, D Day. On the European front we heard that the allies had invaded Europe and, although happy, we wished we could get more help out here, feeling that we were not getting the praise nor backup we deserved. Helped by airdrops of food and ammunition, we moved on down the Imphal Road and within hours arrived at Imphal. Imphal was a small town with a British base, airstrip and tented hospital. It was situated on the Imphal Plains, an oval, somewhat bowl shaped high plateau, surrounded by mountain ranges of woodland, thigh high grass and jungle. In the monsoon season the plains would flood and look like a huge lake enclosed by the mountains.

We headed for a rest area before pushing forward to clear the Silchar Track, another area the Japs occupied. This track left the Imphal Road and went into the mountains, curving back onto the Imphal Road towards the plain of Imphal, flat lands of paddyfields with the roadway itself built up high above them. Nagas and local tribesmen, mostly women, were on the roadside selling fruit and vegetables in big bamboo plaited baskets, dressed in their traditional red pattern, almost Indian style blanket, draped over their shoulders, their black plaited pigtails hanging down from either side of their bronze coloured faces. Their Wild West appearance was completed by the feather in their hair and trailing earrings. The men carried a shotgun or a spear and most had a tinderbox with a flint and would often light our cigarettes for us after the rain had soaked through our clothes, ruining our matches. We reached the rest site and stayed there for a day or so and were issued with monsoon capes before we moved up into some high mountains around the Silchar Track. The monsoon season was starting with sudden downpours of rain and spells of sunshine in the day. It seemed like there was more rain after dark but it was just the same I suppose really, wet and dry spells. As the monsoon continued, the rains lashed at the mountains causing landslides. Lorries slid all over the place and those towing guns were almost impossible to control. Often we would help keep guns connected to the vehicles and on the road by holding onto ropes whilst the driver wrestled with the steering wheel.

In the early hours we moved over the open grassy mountainsides with a lot of dead ground dropping away out of sight. It was a land of streams and ravines with very few trees and slippery, greasy long grass, about eighteen inches high. These were days of never being dry and having permanently wet feet. We would sleep in wet clothes and blankets with water running underneath us as we dozed. Small leeches would wave backwards and forwards on the tips of this grass and many found a place inside our army boots by slipping through the lace holes. They would suck our blood but we didn't feel them as they were crushed in our socks and only discover the tell tale blood stains in our shoes and socks when they were removed. It was the fear of our unknown future that made us take little heed of our discomfort. We almost accepted it all as a part of the life we were leading; eating, sleeping and most of all, trying to stay alive. We longed to hear those magic words, "Leave in India." We would sit on guard each night, on the edge of our trench, half filled with water, ourselves drenched by the monsoon rains and just let our minds drift. It would be two in the morning and my thoughts would go back to Birmingham. Our time zone was five hours ahead and I would think of what was happening at home: Dad would be getting his last pint of beer to take home from the outdoor before it shut. Mom would be preparing supper. Then I would sing a song to myself until, suddenly, I heard a noise. My whole body tensed up and I readied myself, slipping off the safety catch of my rifle and dropping up to my knees in our water filled trench, staring into the darkness. I thanked God it was warm as standing in that water for up to two hours at a time on guard duty would have been unbearable otherwise. I relaxed as all remained quiet and waited to be relieved so I could get some sleep. But sleep was for only two hours as my next stint was at four in the morning, at which time we would have to stand to, in case of a dawn attack. Then it would be a quick breakfast of soya sausage links and beans; help load the mules and off again, marching forward towards the Imphal Road.

I was twenty four years old now, but felt a hundred. All of us young men had seen too much in too short a time. I believe they called it living a lifetime in a day. I don't know about that but what we had seen during the last few months was enough for anyone. Home seemed far away, just a dream. Fatigue would take over, causing confusion. Was this a dream or was this home. You didn't really know but you couldn't let these thoughts take over and so, took a grip, forcing them out of your mind. You brought in new ones like a meal at Firpos when the leave that we longed for so much eventually came through. Then suddenly another noise would be heard and the tension returned. I would become a soldier again, no time for thinking.

Our officers in the lead must either have had a guide or worked from a map and compass as we climbed up the mountainside. The greasy mud covered the wet grass making the climb harder for us soldiers weighed down with extra rations, ammunition and grenades and our rifles. Bill Cordwell was with us. He was in MT (Motor Transport) Section. He had driven lorries in France and the Middle East. It was mules here. The mules carried, boxes of ammunition, tents, bedding, cooking equipment and all the other things to keep a busy army unit in action. In spite of their heavy loads they were sure footed on the grassy slopes and some soldiers hung on to their tails to heave themselves up the steepest parts. Many of us could not bring ourselves to do this. The poor mules had enough weight to carry without us adding to their troubles. I don't know what we would have done without them. They brought us the supplies that were dropped further back by the American and British planes.

We rested where we stood and just lay down to sleep in our monsoon capes in the pouring rain. The mules weren't unloaded and just stood there. We only had a couple of hours sleep or rest; no meals or tea - nothing. I felt sorry for all of us, more so the mules, but we grabbed what rest we could and soon were on our way. The column of men and mules left in a long single line along the narrow muddy rain lashed, leech infested track. We were so tired and past caring about being hungry and wet as the rainwater poured down our steel helmets and monsoon capes, onto our uniform. When daylight came the hot sunshine dried us out but, more important, dried our blankets.

When we arrived near the peaks of the mountains, we went along the Silchar Track for a few miles and spread out in defensive positions. We crossed a deep dry chaung, more a ravine really, with little or no water in it, as there was not much rain now. The early monsoon seemed to have stopped except for the odd shower. We took up our position on a large peak. There were only a few trees around and those were not so high as some we had passed earlier. The Japs had dug bunkers under them. We made our BHQ and Company HQ position and settled in by the track. Others spread out overlooking the ravine. Thankfully C Company were to the rear, a few hundred yards behind BHQ and HQ Company. Other companies were at the front and in flanking positions on the dead ground which sloped away. The rain, when it came, didn't seem as heavy so I didn't wear my monsoon cape on my runs to my Company. Most runs were now straightforward. I crossed to a nearby ravine and along a well-worn track sloping downwards at the bottom of the ravine. Then through the wild bushes and small tree growth that grew either side of a little track and continued down this long gentle slope to a dry riverbed that was full of bushes and trees. I followed this as it wound its way to find it widened as I climbed out the other side, being thirty feet deep at that point. This was a dangerous place that could hide many Japs. The idea of being at the bottom should any Japs appear was frightening. I did my runs and didn't hang around, taking messages as fast and as carefully as I could. All went well for a few days until one day, I slowed down when I heard noises in the chaung. I moved quietly forward creeping but lowering myself to a prone position near the edge of the ravine, my rifle at the ready. To my relief I saw three wild pigs, a mother sow and a large boar male pig with a little young piglet, all snorting and rooting around in the bushes of the bottom of the ravine. I took aim at the male boar pig but decided against firing, thinking OK I could shoot a pig, but someone may get edgy on the hill and if I miss, the bullet would whine around and could draw fire from anyone, comrades or enemy alike. Anyway, odd Jap groups or patrols could have been drawn to any rifle fire. The pigs made my mind up for me. Getting my scent, they raced off at speed into the bushes squealing and grunting. I moved down the ravine and out again and returned to BHQ. When I got back I told them about the pigs and they were not pleased. They felt that a nice bit of pork would have made a welcome change from our normal rations.

Before we moved forward I was sent to bring the officers of the other companies to BHQ for briefing and to study mud maps. These were fascinating. Someone made a mud model of the surrounding terrain and the CO would tell the officers how and when we would move forward.

Another time coming back from a run to my company I heard a cart or a gun being moved. The rattle of wheel noises was in the dead ground near an old Jap position but the terrain hid whoever it was from my sight. I moved up to the side of a peak with the Jap bunkers on top to get a better look and from there I thought I could spot or fire at this hidden gun. As the noise got nearer and nearer from the dead ground I suddenly knew that I wouldn't reach the bunkers in time, they were too high up. It was clear to me that they would see me first on the open high ground, so I stopped and stayed where I was for a few minutes. I nervously waited and let the Japs continue on their way, both of us hidden from each other's view and then calmly, moved down the track and went back to my company BHQ on the hill. The next day after taking a message to my company I had good news. My leave had come through and they gave me a list of places in India that I could visit. This was my first leave in over six months in action and I set off with several other men from my unit to the hill station at Simla. That run was to be my last action on the Silchar Track for, after my leave, I was to rejoin my unit on their advance down the Tiddim Road.

CHAPTER 7

Simla was over two thousand miles from where we were and to get there we had to travel overland. We went to the Indian border and then into India itself, starting with a six hour hike down the mountain sides, the monsoon already having started. To add to our difficulties we were handed a Bren gun to take back for repair to be left at the Admin. Company somewhere on the Imphal Plains near the road. A guide led us, slipping, sliding and falling down the mountainsides, crossing fast flowing mountain streams of white water that made it so hard to keep our balance. Although the streams were narrow, we made slow progress to the other side because of the strong current. High above in the mountains, we looked down on the Imphal plains with clusters of villages and palm trees dotted all over them. The paddyfields were now flooded and looked like one big lake with the mountains rising all around, stretching into the far distance and out of sight. We moved down to meet the lorry which was waiting for us to arrive and would take us to Admin Company then we took another lorry to Dimapur railway station. We wasted no time getting aboard. We were covered in mud. When we saw the Quartermaster at Admin. Company we got a change of uniform and socks and money for our leave as well as passes for the trains. We stayed overnight there and got a lorry to Dimapur station the next morning after breakfast. Our group were put under a Scotch NCO from a West African Regiment. He was an easy going tall Scot who had seen action in the Arakan with the tall African soldiers of the West African Division.

While we waited for our train, we chatted to him and exchanged stories. The station was packed full of soldiers in jungle green. We stood around in groups chatting with our bedding rolls and packs on the ground near us when a strange soldier appeared. He was thick set, in a KD (khaki drill) light off white style of uniform, a pre-war peace time uniform that you saw in some of the Indian garrison towns far from the front line. He sported a silver knobbed cane and marched up to us and started telling us how smart his old regiment was. He told us how on parade you had to be smart and march properly and showed us how by marching up and down. The Scotch NCO grinned and winked at us. He knew what this chap was up to and nodded at two Red Caps (Military Police). This strange soldier stood out like a sore thumb in our crowd of jungle green uniforms. The Red Caps marched him away.

Our tins of rations arrived and we loaded them on to the train with the tea, sugar and tins of milk for making tea along the way and went to our seats. We didn't know it then, but this journey would end at the Brahmaputra River several hours away. From the train, we got onto an old paddle steamer that looked like something out of the old Mississippi western films, so did we with our bush hats and bedding rolls slung over our shoulders. The officers had their pistols on their hips, some tied down in holsters on their thighs, like the old-fashioned gunslingers. To me the whole scene was like a picture out of the comic magazines I used to read as a kid. It was almost unreal. We found a space on the deck and lay out our ground sheet and blanket to rest, using our pack as a pillow. We had no rifles and our small pack had our mess tins, knife, fork and spoon and tin mug for tea. A cooked meal was prepared for us at least once a day on the boat and we still had plenty of tinned food in our ration tins and hot tea for in-between times. We had plenty of cigarettes to smoke and lazy days to get some welcome sleep. There were no guards and we relaxed as the boat made its way. The river was very wide, perhaps a mile or so across and was flooded with the monsoon rains. Now and then the paddle steamer blasted off its horn warning other boats. The echo of that sound gave the feeling of vast space around us, the river was so big and so were the fish. Now and then we would look over the side and see very large black fish of some kind, that, when hearing the steamer coming, sank below the surface some yards in front of us. We took it easy whilst we could and forty eight hours later we reached our destination, another rail head, and boarded the train to Calcutta. Somehow I caught a cold on this train. It seemed the lazy style of life allowed the dormant germs to force their way out but I soon recovered. We still took our daily mepacrine tablets to keep malaria at bay, our skin now turning yellow with their continual use. When we arrived, we settled into the army rest camp of bashas with their typical Indian wooden string beds with coconut fibre mattresses. An organised cook-house gave us meals three times a day. The camp had an M.O. and all the mod cons, even pay parades.

After booking in we later left to visit the Chowringee. We had waited a long time for this. The Chowringee was a main road of hotels, picture houses, barbers and other places of amusement. Most of us went to Firpos Hotel as it was said to be the place to go. A door with the name 'Firpos' above, guided us up a large staircase into a large long room with rows of tables and chairs in typical English style, with snowy white linen table-cloths. It was a right posh affair. We were ushered to tables, each with a waiter and bearer wearing white turbans and clean white tunic style coats and red sashes. They handed us the menus and we settled down to a meal of duck with green peas and potatoes, washed down with a few bottles of ice-cold beer. We spoilt ourselves rotten. Afterwards we went into an air-conditioned picture house. As we sat in comfort I noticed a shelf was provided in front of the seats for the cold drinks and these were sent to us as we sat down watching the film. We even went to an old fashioned barber's shop for a haircut, shave and hot face towels. We couldn't believe it. It was like something out of the old cowboy films. But I had waited a long time for this and remembered my thoughts as we were trapped in our trenches at Kohima. I was determined to enjoy it. I realised how uncertain the future was and seized the moment. The Japs couldn't take this away.

However, outside this luxury, beggars would sit around in the street begging for money and we gave them a few annas of change before continuing on our way to join a mass of other sightseeing soldiers, watching the rickshaw wallahs ply for trade and other street traders with all sorts of things to sell. It seemed that the soldiers of a dozen nations were here, Yanks, British, Indians everyone, both airforce and army. Some men took a chance to go out of bounds to visit prostitutes. Many got away with it, not catching anything, but most stayed in the designated areas.

It was here that I realised that the world was a small place. I met a chap who lived round the corner from us in Birmingham. He was in some other mob somewhere else along the Burma front line. It amazed me that I could meet a person half way across the world although he lived so close to me at home. I never saw him again.

From Howra railway station we left to go to New Delhi where for a few coins the local children helped carry our packs and bedding rolls. We boarded our train and got into the carriages distinctly marked in white letters, BORS (British Other Ranks) and after two days arrived at another rest camp to meet our next train. We had to wait a further three days before it came. Two days and two trains later we arrived at New Delhi.

We asked the RTO Officer when the next train left for Simla and found we would have a day to look round New Delhi before catching an overnight train. New Delhi was more organised than we had experienced elsewhere, a far cry from the hurly-burly of Calcutta. After our day around the town, we boarded the mountain train to Simla. Once aboard, our bearer said that breakfast would be served at four in the morning. We were woken up with a slice of toast, pot of tea, sugar, milk and hot water, all on a neat tray. Quite a change from having breakfast sitting on the floor of the jungle or at the bottom of a trench, rushing to eat it before someone wanted a hand to load a mule or the order came to stand to.

When we reached Simla, we left the train and met the lady in whose bungalow we were staying. We handed over thirty rupees each, for our stay for the following two weeks. Whilst relaxing we discussed and daydreamed of the chances of the monsoon and the wet climate giving rise to landslides, causing the road and rail services to be disrupted so that we could stay extra weeks while repairs took place - wishful thinking!

In Simla we got the same warning about staying in pairs as we had at other hill stations, about the high roads and overhanging cliffs with the possibility of attack by panthers and other wild animals. All around were pine forests and these stretched towards the wild land around the distant snow clad mountains, miles away in the background. We could look over a small wall and look down a deep slope at the treetops of the pine forest. The big light grey monkeys were as surprised as we were to see each other and would leap and bound through the treetops chattering continuously.

The next morning the lady with the bungalow said we could have as much buttered toast and tea as we liked and we should just call the Indian bearer or servant to get it for us. We had already sampled a bowl of the native form of porridge with milk and sugar. It was horrible. We found a small Indian shop between the bungalow and the town that served English food and bacon, eggs, bread, tea and coffee. So each day, after a piece of toast and a cup of tea, we went here for a full English breakfast. Then we would walk around the town and make our way to the bazaar to do some souvenir shopping. At the bazaar you could buy gifts or clothes to send home and there was even a place to get photos taken of ourselves. I had one taken and sent it home to my mother. I also bought a new bush jacket, trousers and side hat in KD creamy brown. The bush jacket had long sleeves to roll up during the day or to bring down at night to protect my arms from the mosquitoes. All this cost only thirty rupees and with free alterations, fitted and ready to collect in two hours.

Simla was a mountain hill station where the Europeans in India sent their families, in the very hot months of the Indian summer before the monsoon broke. The cooler evenings there, the English summer conditions and the clear clean air blowing from the snow covered mountains made it a place for a welcome relaxation, together with its English style churches, bungalows and restaurants. Typical evenings out would be a visit to the picture house followed by a meal afterwards. During our stay we were invited to Vice Regal Lodge with silver thrones, for the Viceroy and his lady. They weren't there themselves and other people were in charge when we arrived. They passed us over to guides who showed us around. These were the native servants and bearers. They were thickset Sikhs of military bearing, dressed up in their regal red tunic style uniforms with gold coats of arms embroidered on the chests, beautiful gold sashes and gold and red turbans,

We were shown around the throne room and admired the large padded armchair style silver thrones. Our uniformed guide trusted us to look around on our own and left us alone for a while and many of us took the opportunity to try out the silver throne chairs for size. Soon we became bored of looking round the room and our servant guide took us to a large lounge where we had tea and a chat with the relatives and friends of the Viceroy. They introduced us to a dancing troop of English and Anglo-Indian can-can dancers that were to dance for us. We felt like Royalty being treated so well by these upper class people.

Unfortunately, our leave passed all too soon and we were back on the train to the front line. On the way back we stopped at a rest camp. The rest camp was hot and dusty, not like the McPherson Barracks at Allahabad, with its modern football and hockey pitches and tennis courts. There, we had the luxury of being shaved in bed in the early morning and our kit cleaned with a fresh change of uniform twice a day, morning and evening, all delivered by the laundry man or Dhobi as he was called. It was neatly placed at the end of our beds, boots polished, ready to wear. There was even a barber and a tailor there and we had hand made shoes for the evening wear. We had the life of gentlemen and would relax with our charwallah, (tea and cakes), and a fruitwallah on the veranda outside. This place was distinctly different and nowhere near as comfortable. Simple bashas provided our accommodation with rough covered separate toilets and shower blocks.

Soon after we got there we met our old friendly NCO, who had originally come out from England to India with us. He was wounded at Kohima and his wound got him a downgrade from the infantry and a safe job on the rest camp. He was still one of the lads and looked after us arranging a pay parade. We hadn't been paid for weeks. He told us that there was another train later that week so we didn't have to rush, arranging for us to have an extra day or two at the rest camp, away from the front line. We followed the same route back by train to Calcutta and train again, followed by the paddleboat. It all seemed to have gone so fast. We arrived at the jetty to disembark to get the train back to Dimapur. We had a further night in a rest camp there and then continued back through Kohima and Imphal and on to BHQ.

Milestone 143, Tiddim Road

CHAPTER 8

By now the Japs were well on the run. Many dead or dying not from death or glory charges, but from disease and starvation as it was their turn to retreat and be trapped. The Silchar track had now been cleared of the Japs and we returned to continue our advance down the Tiddim Road some miles past Imphal. I was still retained as C Company Runner. After returning from leave I was apprehensive. There was no easy way back into the job. The monsoon was still in full swing and I started by doing a run the next day. The mud was so deep it covered my boots. I had to travel from our BHQ roadside mountain defensive positions to the forward position of my company, which was along a trail deeper in the mountains. The roads were thick with liquid mud and again the lorries struggled, but this time there was no room for error as there was a sheer drop at the road edge.

We had a rest while another battalion took the lead for a few days and received some canteen goods, extra canned fruit and a bottle of beer. The cooks prepared some dehydrated potatoes, onions and mutton for the last hot meal of the day. We washed that down with a mug of hot tea. Then we took our mepacrine tablet to ward off malaria and our rum ration using our mugs. As darkness fell the guards were set for the night. No sudden attacks were expected but we still stood to in our trenches. Thousands of Japs were falling back in retreat and were scattered all over the place. We still couldn't take any chances. Some of us were allowed to stand down, but others remained at their posts. We took our turn later, the trenches now had six inches of water in the bottom. The two man tents were pitched on a level piece of ground we scraped out near the slit trench we'd dug. These tents were carried on mules during the day as we advanced, but provided us shelter when resting in between stints of guard duty at night. As dawn broke we would wash and shave as there was no shortage of water now. The monsoon made sure of that and we got ready to move on. We travelled more than three hundred miles over parts of a road where battles, past and new, had left bodies in varying states of decay; some fresh, others just bones. As the road changed with the terrain of valleys and mountains, we approached the Manipur River. At that time I shared the two man tent with a Scot from Edinburgh. A quiet man with a middle class accent. I liked him, we got on fine. I would moan about this and that and he would agree. We didn't fall out or upset each other and that was important.

After we'd captured Tiddim, our next target was the Third Stockade further up the Tiddim Road. This was a Japanese supply base where they kept their food stores, with sacks of rice, a form of cocoa powder, tins of mixed meat, cherries amongst other things. We had to capture this place to break the supply lines to the Japanese defences. Tiddim was at the end of the Chocolate Staircase, a road built up the side of a mountain in loops of hairpin bends, seemingly taking the form of a large staircase. This and the sickly reddish-brown coloured mud gave it its nickname. Behind that was a well defended high mountain top called Kennedy Peak. From here the Japanese could view the road for miles. That had to be captured too.

In front of us, was a twenty mile 'bush' typhus belt, a real concern to the West African Division. The British troops seemed to recover better from this illness. Many of the West Africans died. They were superstitious of these tropical diseases and would give up the fight to live. It was said that it was caught from a rat bug or flea that lived on the tips of the long grass and that these attacked the bare arms unprotected by the rolled up sleeves in the hot climate of the jungle. We were given oil to rub into our arms everyday, to protect us and were ordered to keep the long sleeves of our jungle green tunics down, but some still caught it. Swarms of small flies would suddenly rise in clouds at dusk. They got everywhere. They bit your backside if you went to the toilet. I made sure I didn't go then. They even got under your helmet and didn't half make your head itch. They only came out in the early evening, no other time. They disappeared as quickly as they appeared. We were glad when we left them behind.

We moved out in sections, either side of the road passing bloated dead bodies of Japanese stragglers. Sick and ill, they died where they fell at the side of the road. The smell of the death was with us all the time as we passed rotting bodies, friend or foe, you couldn't tell really, just some bones in a uniform, unrecognisable by now.

As we pushed on I met Preston. He lived around the corner at home, in Birmingham and was married with a small child. He joined us and when we stopped to strike camp we talked about home. I remember that he always sang one particular song, one that he sang to his wife - 'Bless you for being an Angel.' It was his favourite and he often sang it whilst putting up the tent or during the singsongs we used to have. He was killed later, shot in error by one of our own chaps with a Sten gun. It was terrible. These guns were always a problem, often jamming or firing after the slightest jolt. Many a time a dispatch rider would ride his motorcycle over a bump in the road to hear the sound of the automatic machine gun fire, only to realise it was his own weapon. Poor Preston however, had been standing in front of a bloke cleaning his gun when it went off for no apparent reason. He was caught with a short burst of bullets to the stomach.

We halted for a night near the riverbanks of the Manipur River and dug in and pitched our tents. We were to cross it next day. There was no bridge. We heard the roar of the fast flowing river long before we saw it. The floodwater was sand coloured, white in places, showing its strength by juggling the tree logs floating down it. A boat appeared from somewhere and some Indian soldiers used to the flooded rivers managed to swim over with a cable to help bring the boat across. I don't know how they managed it. The current was horrendous. The rope or cable they took with them was wrapped round a thick tree trunk on the bank on the other side and a group of our soldiers boarded the boat and work commenced to pull it across. Part of the way over, the boat tipped over and the men fell into the river. It was chaos as the vicious current washed the poor men away. Quite a few were missing and patrols were sent to search the banks. Some were found with broken arms where large rocks dragged down by the flooded waters had smashed into them. Those were lucky ones, the others drowned. My little friend from Scotland was in that boat and was missing, presumed drowned. His body was never found. The water had risen above the side of the boat as they pulled it across, flooding it and causing it to tip.

I was detailed to go on the second boat and hoped that the people in charge had learnt their lesson. We took no chances and took our gaiters off so that if the water went into our trousers it would not be caught by them. We carried all our packs and pouches but they were loose ready to throw off for us to swim for it to the banks should the boat capsize. I had an awful feeling of being expendable but didn't show it. We all got in the boat and as we waited I said a little prayer. The boat slowly moved across the river and, as we got nearer the middle, the water started to climb higher and higher up the sides. It was only inches from the top, but to our relief it slowly dropped again. The rest of the group crossed safely during the next few hours.

On the other side I discovered a group of dead Japs in an open space about thirty or forty feet from the riverbank. They were long dead, just bones. I picked up a small ivory rod around three inches long, it looked thick like a pen. It was a Japanese family name stamp and I kept it for a souvenir. When everybody was finally across we moved away from the river. Soon, the river became like a silver thread of cotton behind us, weaving its way through the mountains. In front of us the road turned into a large horse-shoe shape and we moved into a position covered with jungle and long grass along the mountainside overlooking the road. We went forward into Japanese held territory. It was four in the afternoon and I was sent on a run with a message to my Company, having to return in the dark through unknown enemy held territory. I didn't like that.

We were told that some women bearers were to help us carry our equipment. We were excited until they turned up. They were "old hags" in their fifties led by an old man. They were good bearers though.

There were breaks in our advance down the road and whilst dug in on a mountainside, overlooking the road another infantry unit passed through the mountains and around us to take the lead. We were told that we would be resting where we were for a few days. That suited us. We received some mail and made sure we got some rest and sleep. We also took the opportunity to write letters. Some got parcels from home and local papers. We also got more to eat and a bottle of beer from the airdrop area. These were brought up by mules and lorries which worked relentlessly in the pouring monsoon rains. In the evening we had our rum ration and went through the routine of taking our malaria tablets and rubbing our ointment into our arms to protect us from typhus. In the daytime we took life easy when we could and on one occasion I walked round and looked at a group of mules, tethered to a clump of trees, feeding. They seemed to see me or at least sense me watching. I was perhaps too close to them and they moved almost as one bringing their rear ends slowly in my direction, as if to warn me. I kept my distance as the last thing I needed was one of them to lash out with its back legs and injure me. I realised that they needed time and space as well so I left them in peace. That evening, Japs started shelling the land near our rest area, reminding us they were still out there and knew where we were. We moved out the next day.

I was still C Company Runner and my work was never done. It seemed harder travelling from this rest area in the mid-afternoon, but that was the time I got my orders, to take a message to my forward Company. It was a long hike down the muddy main road with dozens of hairpin bends, the jungle growing thicker and thicker near the recesses in the curves of the road, fed by the little watercourses that trickled down the hillside. I could smell death all the time and found a fresh corpse of a Japanese soldier that was not there the day before. I found his rifle first, on the road and moved into the jungle to find his discarded pack, then the Jap's body. His head was hanging down over a stream. I wasn't sure he was dead at first and approached carefully, but he was. The Japs diet was mainly rice and they sometimes drank too much water, which caused the rice they'd eaten to swell and kill them. I left after throwing the rifle over the sheer drop into the bushy jungle beneath to prevent it being used again. I left the body where it was.

Our advance continued and a muddy mound rose in the road. Stretchers and parts of an ambulance, skulls, helmets, bones and uniforms were all embedded in the mud with our transport still going over it, as we chased the retreating enemy that had not the time to clear the road properly or bury their dead. It was a sickly, awful sight. The mud was baked hard in places with bits of body sticking out of it. A British bulldozer was called in to do the job some weeks later, clearing away the stinking mound of bodies but, meanwhile, I had to climb over them.

I would deliver my messages and try to get back to BHQ before it got dark. But I never did. It was always dark before I reached this mound of death. I knew I was close by the smell and although I had done this journey many times in the dark, I was always nervous. Whether it was the place I don't know, but I always had my rifle ready with my finger on the trigger, ready to blast any Jap I saw in front of me. It was a lonely road in the dark and I would be lucky if I saw anyone on my runs. It was a very dangerous area too and there was plenty of opportunity for the enemy to ambush me at every deep jungle covered curve and crevice, in the dark corners of mountain bends. On the top of all this I had to remember the password when challenged by the guards at BHQ, hoping they would remember me being out there and not be trigger-happy. I would arrive at BHQ and the guards would challenge me, demanding the password. They knew it was me. They recognised my shape and voice but used to pretend they had not heard. I repeated the password, this time louder. "Speak louder next time," one of the guards would say. It was all a little game they played to break up the monotonous hours of guard duty. They'd heard me the first time and I'd swear at them as I passed through with them laughing quietly. I couldn't do much about it. I couldn't blunder through without giving the password. They could have shot me.

We came across a part of the road that had dropped. A landslide had caused it. About one hundred yards of the road was gone. I had to climb over the mud and shale slope of the landslide and back onto the road again to take my messages to the forward positions. They got two bulldozers working on it, one from each end and soon shaped a new road on the site of the landslide and got the traffic of war on the move once again. As the battalion advanced, the pouring rain continued to fall. The mud was so deep that it covered our boots and lorries found it difficult to keep on a straight course with a sheer drop to the one side of the road. Ropes were used to stop the gun supports, attached to the lorries, going over the edge. You wouldn't get them back if they went over. They'd be lost down the sheer drop in the jungle beneath. Despite the weather, we could still hear the droning sound of the American Curtis Commandos and Dakotas, cargo planes, dropping supplies further back. We would have been at a loss without these planes and appreciated their support. They operated whatever the weather.

One day I left the road and climbed into the mountains following a track which led to a native Chinn village. High on an outcrop of rocky land were stone built huts with thatched roofs. They had no doors or windows, just rectangular openings. Nearby I noticed a fruit tree with large fruit, like green skinned oranges. I decided against going in to the deserted village. It seeming too risky at the time but I took half a dozen oranges and put them inside my tunic and continued to C Company's position further along the track. Here two badly wounded chaps were under a rough shelter with their stretchers off the ground. Both were well wrapped up and protected against the rain. They would need mules to get them out. It was a shame and I wondered if they'd make it. On my return journey I had to take some sick chaps back to BHQ. They weren't that bad and were mobile enough to travel unaided. One of the chaps was called Ingram and I knew him. I gave them some of my oranges to suck, cutting them in half and although sour and bitter they ate them. I didn't rush them and took a slow walk back, allowing them rest wherever possible. It was a dicey track if you were fit let alone ill and there were lots of stray Japs about. As we moved back, I was not too happy about that deserted Chinn village with the orange tree growing near the track. I made them rest for a few minutes while I scouted around the two dangerous bends in the track that could hide an ambush. I went into the jungle bush and worked my way round the back to check that no-one was lying in wait. All was clear and we slowly went forward, going down the open track on the mountainside to BHQ. After the war I met Ingram in Rangoon. He always told others, "Here's the chap who saved my life when I had typhus on the Imphal Road." I would get quite embarrassed.

Our Company was on the move again and we moved along the road to find an old Jap tank out of action. It had been pushed halfway over the drop at the edge of the road. Further along on some flat ground a Jap gun stood idle, its long barrel blown to pieces, sabotaged so it could not be used against them. The smell of death was still with us and more bodies of dead Japs littered both sides of the road, some partly buried in the mud. It was a vile sight. We even found a lorry with a money making, printing machine and thousands of 'Japanese Rupee' notes. They had 'The Government of Japan' written on them. I collected a few clean ones to take home as souvenirs.

It was nearly September as we moved forward, climbing higher. There was still heavy rain. My runs to C Company and back went on, each one becoming longer. When I got the chance I would explore redundant Jap lorries abandoned along the road. I searched for anything of interest, such as information or the odd souvenir.

They were a good lot of chaps, our lot. We all mixed in together, the cockneys, the Welsh and the rest. There was a lad with us called Bernard James and he spent most of his time with his two mates. He was shot in the knee and died. He went into shock and never recovered. We hadn't eaten for two days and that didn't help. We couldn't believe he'd gone through the Arakan, Kohima and the rest and died of shock! Some time later I was coming back from taking a message and I found a cross marking James' grave. I thought I was alone and picked some flowers and laid them by the cross and stood there for a little while. Then a voice said, 'Hello Street.' It was the padre. I felt embarrassed. I don't know where he came from. We were in the middle of nowhere.

Our next objective was in sight. We approached the Chocolate Staircase. Here the road took the form of a staircase as its winding hairpin bends climbed up the mountainside, like steps. Its chocolate coloured mud covered everything right up to the peak. We had some miles to go yet though and halted for a rest. We soon reached and climbed the road up the Chocolate Staircase. The weather got drier with the hot sunshine. We could clearly see the endless ranges of mountains disappearing away in the distance. I was detailed to take another run to my Company now in the frontline, in their the mountain positions. On the way, I saw a Jap half track burnt out. There were no bodies in it and I had a look inside. I found a pistol and leather holster attached to a bullet proof steel side panel and took it out for a look. It was a Luger style pistol or automatic but was too badly burnt to keep as a souvenir, so I left it. Passing through the jungle, I began to notice that the water was drying up in the little clear mountain streams that came from the jungle covered crevices in the loops and bends of the road. It looked like the dry weather was coming to stay.

We all marched up the Chocolate Staircase, the other traffic and guns moving up in lorries and on mules, passing some Indian troops moving down. We didn't know were they were going, but there was a lot of movement of troops going on at that time. During our march we would look out for water supply points along the road, hoping to see or hear some running water. I went down off the road into the thick cover of trees and the bush in the jungle and found a wild banana grove and heard water running. Banana groves were a good clue. Their large leaves would stand out to show water to be around, in this case two hundred yards away down the mountainside. I made a mental note of the distance and place as we marched past. We were now beginning to learn the ways of the jungle.

High up in this high jungle covered mountain we found a site to rest for the coming night. I was detailed to take a mule and another soldier back down to fill the water tanks. We retraced our steps down the road over-looking the banana grove. We moved carefully down, over rocky rough areas between the bushes and trees and arrived amongst the banana trees growing out of the limestone ledges. There was our water supply, pouring into shallow pools on a bed of limestone about two or three inches deep. The place stank. Wild pigs had been foraging and feeding off the rotting bananas and vegetation, churning everything up into a stinking mess. It didn't matter. We slowly filled the water tanks and bottles and returned with the mules to our position before darkness set in.

New orders arrived. We were to go back down to the bottom of the Choco-late Staircase to the main road, take another route and infiltrate eighty miles behind the Japanese lines. This was a covert operation with us leav-ing the road at a secret track and moving through the mountains, valleys, native villages and open countryside. We met with the groups of natives and soldiers that had operated behind the Jap lines. We were going to give the Japs a shock in the days ahead as we had brought in a battery of moun-tain guns on the mules with skilled Indian mountain battery gunners and officers. The Japs intended to make a stand at the high point on the Tiddim Road called Kennedy Peak where they would have a good view of our oncoming troops. If they could, this would give the rest of the Jap forces time to cross the Chindwin River and get into Burma some miles away. There, they could organise air transport and supplies and give them time to clear their stores and regroup on the other side. Our job was to cut the road behind Kennedy Peak and trap the Japs with their transport. We marched at night and holed up in the daytime close to the Japanese posi-tions. The weather was unrelenting as we pushed forward, unloading the mules before first light, digging in and then trying to get some sleep be-tween stints of guard duty. The noise of the insects and jungle creatures made sleeping difficult. In the late afternoon we would reload the mules and be on the march again in the early evening. We passed through many Chinn villages, their typical houses on stilts and decorated with buffalo horns. That was unusual to us. One house that belonged to a Catholic priest had an English style lawn with a water tap and stood out from the rest. That was a real surprise, finding something like that in the middle of the mountains. We continued marching, night after night. In places the tracks were so narrow, the mules would scrape their loads against the cliff face causing them to become nervous of the drop on the other side. They would kick and buck as the muleteers struggled to control them. It was hard as the animals were chained together in threes. If one bucked it was likely all three would become upset, kicking out in an attempt to lose their load. We did lose three mules. The lead mule bucked and panicked and fell over the side, dragging the other two with it. We all watched in horror as the helpless creatures plunged down into the darkness. A group of men and muleteers were sent to retrieve what they could and returned with some of the loads that could be used, but the poor mules perished. We pushed on higher and higher up the mountains realising that the only way home now was forward. It was on this march that I tripped over a small rock on the track, catapulting me over and down the side of the road. Fortunately I didn't fall too far. I was carrying a full pack and equipment and the sudden jolt winded me for a while. I got up and continued, but never seemed to be up to the pace after that.

One night at the head of our long line of men, amongst the high pine forest ridges that flanked the track, our CO and Officer stopped to look at the maps more closely with their pencil torch. We had come too far and were in a very dangerous area. The order to halt came and BHQ and HQ Company moved into the wooded ridges to the left of the mountain track and we prepared to drop back. On the way, we came across a British officer with Indian tribesman soldiers, making the mountain track wide enough to take jeeps. It was incredible that they were working in this dangerous No Mans Land. Nearby we noticed a dead body of a Jap, only a few days old, sprawled over some bushes. We moved past him and the working party and left them to get on with their work. We holed up in a pine forest for a few days. Things didn't go to plan. The Japs soon knew we were behind them. They tried to delay us and we soon found that there were many more Japs and transport retreating down the Tiddim Road than we had realised. This was more than our small group of men could handle. We were only sent to mine the road, blow up lorries and then go back to base. We returned to BHQ, dug in near the track with our rifle company flanking us, with C Company to the rear and awaited further orders.

The runs were sometimes twice a day taking messages to and from my Company. I would go out in the late afternoon and return in darkness. It wasn't the same as past runs. This time I was eighty miles behind the Jap lines, in virgin forest. Then I had to find my own way back to BHQ in the pitch-black darkness. That was really hard up there in the pine forest.

There were no proper tracks. We had made those that existed. It was all right during the day as I could recognise trees and shapes or surrounding high and low points but in the darkness it was impossible. I only just about made it back the first time after going into a small clearing in the forest to get a better idea of direction. It was more by luck than judgement that I came into an open area with fewer trees and found BHQ. I had been lost.

Fortunately, on leave I bought a bone handled Ghurkha knife, suitable to cut sapling trees down or use as a weapon. It came in very handy as I took my message the next day. I moved into the forest a few yards and blazed a new trail. Not a trail for daylight use, as a Jap patrol could follow it to our camp. So I missed the first few trees and facing a tree trunk I went behind it and took a slice out, going down about a foot, leaving a light patch. I missed out a further three trees and repeated this again, several times, until I reached a small clearing. This was another reminder of the comics I used to read as a kid about the old Wild West. The frontier folk cutting trails into the unknown.

Almost out of the forest and in open land, with a few pines marked up near my Company position, I delivered the message. When it got dark, I re-entered the wood in the same place. Leaving the small clearing I found the first tree and retraced my tracks back to camp. It wasn't easy. I found it difficult having to go back to the marked trees to get my directions. I eventually arrived at our camp and was passed through by the guard. By my third night I managed to make my way back in the dark quite easily, finding the marker trees a lot more quickly.

We felt our positions must be very near the Tiddim Road as there were telephone poles and wire near our camp. We were ordered to cut those wires going to the Jap lines and half a dozen of us set off, including some signallers, with pairs of pincers. They supplied us each with pistols. We left our rifles behind to travel light and set off for a telegraph pole in a hollow on the forest floor overlooked by high ridges all around. One of the chaps went up the telegraph pole and found the wire was half an inch thick. It was hard going cutting it with the small pincers and seemed to take forever. As we finished we saw a patrol, high on a ridge above. They were too far away to see who they were so we took cover behind some trees. We got our pistols at the ready to fire. If they were the enemy, they would be out of range for our pistols, but we would be in the range of their rifles. As they got closer we were relieved to see that they were ours. We got a surprise when they told us that we would have been dead ten minutes earlier if they had been the enemy. They had been watching us as we cut the telephone wire.

It was nearly October and there was a kind of winter here on these high peaks. We stood to in our slit trench in a foggy cold morning mist. We heard the heavy explosions of Jap shells somewhere in the valley below. We couldn't see anything because of the mist. If they were aiming at us they were well off target and we were thankful that they couldn't see us. The shelling ceased and we heard no more. Our front rifle Companies had made contact with the Japs and we heard the battle going on as our mountain guns opened fire in support. The noise soon quietened and we remained where we were. The next day we made our way down to the road on to some flat land, to camp near a river by an old Japanese position. There were some Jap graves with wooden marker posts, with Jap writing on them. Nearby a small river ran on a gravel bed and I decided to have a quick wash. I found a lump in my left side and went to see the MO. I'd got a hernia, probably when I fell of the track, half asleep with exhaustion, during a march further back up the mountains. Nothing could be done where we were. I needed surgery but I couldn't leave for hospital as the airstrip was still to be captured. We marched on for a few hours to stay in a teak forest near a former Jap base camp. We rested in our tents at this camp, BHQ was set up near the sandy track. The large high trunks of the teak trees had no low branches. I remember thinking that this was just as well as I noticed a python hanging from one of the higher boughs.

We pitched our tent near this tree, the snake was well out of the way up there. However, in the fine sandy tracks around were a mass of snake trails of all sizes. Most of the snakes were small. We hoped they weren't poisonous as to be bitten out here would probably be fatal. This reminded me of a four foot long grass snake with a bright red head, that had surprised me up in the mountains. The snake came out of the bushes and went under a tent wall and I happened to see it as I cleared some ground nearby. I dashed round the other side and cut its head off, with one swing of the spade. I found out later that it was harmless and felt quite guilty for killing the poor reptile. I don't know whether it was because we were constantly surrounded by death. We'd happily shoot the Japs. We had to. But it seemed unnecessary to kill animals for the sake of it.

While we were at this former Japanese camp I took the opportunity to look round. The NCO reminded me to watch out as there may be some Jap stragglers hanging about in the jungle around, so I remained cautious. I saw two natives loading their bullock cart with some of the stores that the enemy had left behind. The cart was full and one of them was on the cart, the other nearby. They looked very worried but I thought they looked Burmese. Their hands were under their gowns. I couldn't see if they had any weapons. My rifle was slung over my shoulder and so I had the choice, of either playing it cool and taking no notice or unslinging my rifle and risk getting killed before capturing them. I decide to play it cool and let them go on their way and continued to look round. The other native quickly jumped on to the bullock cart and they whipped the two bullocks and raced away. I could have shot them for looting but there was no need. I thought good luck to them.

As I looked around I saw some broken Jap rifles amongst the debris. I tried to find one that would work. Looking more closely I saw some half buried paper and gently dug it out. Someone had buried it in a hurry. It turned out to be two military Japanese maps. They were beautifully coloured, showing the sea and coastline of either Burma or China, with neat Japanese writing. They were two feet wide, so I carefully folded them up and put them into my pocket and later handed them in to 'I' Section. I found a rifle not damaged except for the bolt missing and its barrel packed with mud. Nearby some leather pouches of Jap rifle bullets were tipped out on the ground. I got a bolt from another damaged rifle and loaded the weapon. I cleared the rifle barrel with a bullet and moved into the forest to try it out. I fired a few shots at various targets before realising that the noise of an enemy rifle may attract others and returned to camp.

CHAPTER 9

It was October 1944 when the airstrip was captured, I waited for pay parade and went sick the next day, reporting my hernia. Arrangements were made and I was flown to Imphal for treatment. The hospital at Imphal was a large tented hospital but wounded men and urgent cases took priority. It was decided I would be treated elsewhere. After a week I was flown to a hospital in Chittagong, a coastal town near the Bay of Bengal. I spent a further two weeks of relaxation and rest on the sandy beaches nearby, swimming in the warm sea. That was welcome. Eventually, I was taken by hospital ship to Madras and had my operation just before Christmas.

It was at that time they held a commemorative service at Kohima. Some of the Royal West Kents were on the guard of honour. A mate of mine, Ronnie Millward, was there and had his photo taken. His family ran a business as sign writers and decorators. He was a great kid and we used to get him to write letters to our girlfriends because he had such neat and stylish handwriting. Padre Randolph took the service. That was apt. He was of tremendous spiritual support to those that needed it when we were at Kohima. There weren't many that didn't. A teak cross was erected as a memorial. Ivan Daunt and Ernie Stonnell made it. They were sent to Dimapur after the siege to choose some teak and spent hours inscribing each of the dead men's names on it. It stood there for nearly twenty years before being brought back in pieces to England in 1961. Bob Clinch, a pioneer sergeant of HQ Company, meticulously restored it. It is now displayed in the Royal West Kent Museum in Maidstone.

Whilst recovering in hospital I contracted dysentery and malaria. It seemed ironic that I would nearly die of disease after surviving battles of the Arakan, Kohima and the Imphal Road. We lost many through the various tropical diseases. Fortunately I pulled through.

Battalion Memorial

Padre Randolph

Graves at Kohima 1944

Graves at Kohima 1944

Ernie Stonnel and Ivan Daunt working on the Kohima Cross

139

Tennis Court Memorial

Kohima December 1944

In January 1945 Lady Mountbatten visited the hospital. I hadn't long had my operation and was lying flat on my back. I hoped she'd pass by but the nurse or someone must have said I was a member of the Fourth Royal West Kents back from the actions of Kohima and the Imphal Road. Well she made a beeline for me. I wanted to sink through the floor rather than meet her but she smiled and chatted with me asking if I had seen her husband. He was in charge of the South East Asia Command. I said that I had, but told her that every time we did, we went back into action. She went on to tell me how Lord Mountbatten thought the world of us and appreciated all the good work we'd done. Wishing me well and to get better soon, she passed on to chat to the others. Several days later, the ward sister told me that someone had been asking about me and when I asked who it was she said she was not allowed to say but that they were very important. Anyway, she brought me a form to fill in and I was given special leave for a month in England.

I had to wait several weeks before being discharged from hospital. It was April 1945 and I was sent to the convalescence depot sited in the Wellington Hills near Madras. After a couple of weeks of taking it easy and doing light duties such as laying tables, the NCO came to tell me my leave had come through. He added that when I was fit and ready to travel, I could take my one month's home leave. He said I could be downgraded and take an easier job when I returned. When the time came, it took me seventeen days to get back to England. Fortunately, my leave didn't start until I arrived back so I enjoyed VE Day in England before making the seventeen day trip back to Bombay. Arriving home was traumatic. At a family gathering I began to feel so strange. Everything seemed unreal. My parents looked old and grey since I saw them last. Things became confused and I burst into tears. After a few minutes I was all right but it appeared the pressures of the last few months had finally surfaced. My mother got in touch with the local MP complaining that I was not fit enough to return to the front line. They even got an army MO to check me over but he said it was too late for him to do anything about it. He said that I should speak to someone when I got back to arrange for a downgrade and get an easier job in India rather than go back to the front line. I wasn't bothered but my mother was.

I remember on one occasion on home leave, I was on a bus with one of my aunts, laughing and joking. A woman came across saying I shouldn't be acting up like I was. There was a war on and I should be out there fighting. Well, before I knew what was going on, my aunt reared up on her giving her such a dressing down, telling her where I had been and what I had been through. I ended up having to separate the pair of them.

The leave ended all too quickly and I went by train to Glasgow to catch the troopship, 'The Queen of Bermuda' to Bombay. It was horrible when the train started to leave the station. Husbands had just parted from their wives and children in tearful farewells. Some of the poor blokes couldn't bring themselves to speak for a half hour or so. Others were virtually in tears. Us single men left them to thaw out and would joke and mess about, talk about our leave and play cards. The others eventually joined in when they were ready. A mix-up took place in Bombay and instead of having a soft job I was sent back to Calcutta and on to Rangoon, to the front line. It was my own fault really. All the soldiers were lined up waiting to go back to their units when the sergeant asked me which Regiment I was from. I felt I couldn't say that I ought to be going to a convalescence depot, be downgraded and given an easy job, not in front of all these other blokes. So I said I was with the Royal West Kents, hoping to get a chance to sort it all out later but I didn't. In a way though, I was glad to be back in India, feeling free and enjoyed the respect I received from the locals. It was as if I had gone back in time a thousand years. Bullock carts trundled along, high pitched music and singing wailed all around, a sacred cow chewed aimlessly. I loved it for some reason. This was my type of life in the hot dusty climate. It was not like at home. Here people would rush to carry your bag, shine your shoes, sell you fruit and tea and it cost virtually nothing. Even the prospect of an uncertain future seemed part of the adventure. It was confusing really. I couldn't wait to get home and then I wanted the freedom and lifestyle we had out here. It was strange. Anyway, we were sent to Calcutta and then by boat across the Bay of Bengal to Rangoon to go back to the Burma front line. I had not been there before. Rangoon had not long been taken. When we got there my old Signals Sergeant met us. He had been in the Arakan, one of the old members of the West Kents. He'd served in the Middle East before coming to the Arakan. He was at Kohima in the Signals Bunker just a few yards higher than our trench and had served in the front line throughout the months I had been away in hospital and home leave. He said it would be too risky to return to the company that night and so we had a night on the town in Rangoon.

We took the opportunity to visit the sights, one was the Shwedagon Pagoda, a vast complex of statues and hundreds of Buddhas sitting and lying in small temples. It was night and we soldiers wandered round as a group. We could see the priests in their saffron robes, their heads shaved, attending the candlelit shrines. I lit a candle and made my wish and gave the candle to a young Burmese woman with white flowers in her hair. With the thought of impending action, I wished I was home again. After our visit to the pagoda we went to a Chinese restaurant for a meal of lobsters, large prawns, salad and coffee.

SHWEDAGONPAGODA
RANGOON.

The next day our Sergeant drove us very fast out of Rangoon as there were Jap snipers about. We went along the tarmac main road, passing through the flooded paddyfields on either side, driving through the monsoon, only broken by short hot periods of sunshine. As we travelled, we could see clusters of palm trees around villages with people tending their water buffaloes. In the distance I could hear the faint sound of gunfire and began to tense up with that feeling of dread I had experienced before. I knew it would pass when I'd got used to being in action again but it didn't help at that time. We passed through the wayside villages, the huts were on stilts, one even with an open front selling fruit, amazing sights. Eventually we arrived at BHQ, a tented site in a sea of watery mud. It was a gloomy place and thankfully someone else had got my job as runner. I returned to my Company that was in another village in huts on stilts. I was allotted to a hut with some people I knew from the old days but noticed quite a number of new young lads. They filled me in on what was happening. They had been patrolling on a twenty mile area to clear

143

the Jap odds and sods in the local area. The main road was still unsafe to use. Just before I'd arrived, a lorry taking some soldiers back to Rangoon to catch a troopship to England had been ambushed. Several of the men were killed. Now back in a platoon of C Company I joined one of these Jap clearing patrols but only did a couple of sorties before we moved on.

We got transport to the area we were to patrol, cutting down on the marching we did in the previous campaigns. We still had to cross the flooded paddyfields. Some were now drying out but others were flooded with streams flowing through them. We stored our cigarettes and matches in our steel helmets as we waded across. I pitied the non-swimmers and very short people. The water was at least waist deep and rising slowly to over our chests and deeper. We passed the deepest point and climbed out the other side. As we approached one of the villages on higher, drier ground, about a dozen water buffalo with their vast sweeping horns lowered their heads and turned towards us getting ready to charge. We continued to approach the village and our lives, or rather the lives of these buffaloes, depended on a ten year old Burmese lad in charge of them. All he had was a catapult that fired clay stone marbles. The buffaloes begin to form a half circle and start to move forward as if to charge. We stood our ground our automatic weapons ready to fire at about one hundred yards. The young lad saw the danger and started shouting at the buffalos. At the same time he sent clay marbles from his catapult at them to try to stop the charge. It did, saving the animals lives and perhaps the village food supply.

We moved forward and checked out the village for Japs. There didn't appear to be any and the villagers said that there were no Japs in the area. We carried on with our patrol meeting up with some trucks at the pickup point on the road and returned to our base. A large clay urn lay on its side outside our hut. It was about four feet high. Seeing that it could store plenty of water we placed it under the eaves of the thatched pitched roof of our hut. As the waves of the monsoon rain fell the large urn soon filled, past overflowing. We took full advantage and filled our water bottles, washed out our mess tins, washed down our bodies and had a shave. We stayed in the village for several days. I had noticed that some of the huts were empty and had a look around. In one I found a roughly made crossbow but it was broken. I repaired it with a piece of signal wire. I used a six inch nail for a bolt and fired it at a nearby tree. The nail buried itself about an inch into the trunk, making it difficult to get out. I messed around a little longer with my new toy and went back to base.

Some days later 'O' (Operations) Group called and we were given the job of blocking the escape routes of several thousand Japs trapped in the Pegu Yomas. They were dying of disease and starvation and getting ready to try to break out to get to the Siam border, across a main road. We moved towards Pegu travelling by jeep train, the jeep drawing flat top trucks to a railway embankment overlooking a track to the main road. We dug in on the embankment and could see across the flooded paddyfields with the village in the background and one of the escape tracks the Japanese might use to reach Siam, or die of disease or starvation in the low jungle covered hills of the Pegu Yomas. It was our job to patrol along this track and bump into any leading groups of Japs that had started to move out from the main body. As we climbed into the flat top trucks I put on a new bush hat to protect me from the sun but, out on the paddyfields, a gust of wind blew it off. So it was back to the steel helmet.

We lived in the open, rain or shine, spending day and night in our trenches, while we remained in our position to block these escape routes. At the bottom of the railway embankment was a paddyfield, flooded and full of weeds, fish and frogs. I wasn't happy with this position. I thought it would limit the use of grenades if the Japs attacked out of the paddyfield. Here, it was a battle for the Bren, rifle and bayonet. We were told we could call on the support of the air strikes, tanks and artillery, if required. I decided to take things a little further and put out pungies. These were small, short lengths of bamboo stakes in the two foot high grass. I positioned them at forty five degrees, sticking about six inches out of the ground with trip wires hidden amongst them. This was to try to stop any attacking Japs surprising me in the night. If they did come they'd trip and fall onto the pungies, giving me a chance to shoot first.

After two nights on guard we heard splashes in the water of the paddyfield and a sudden silence of the croaking frogs. All was quiet for about five minutes as I strained my eyes, rifle and fixed bayonet ready to beat off any attack. The frogs started up again calling to their mates and we were safe again for the time being. This went on night after night. It was an awful feeling when the frogs and other creatures suddenly went quiet. We stayed very much alert but the enemy never came.

One day we were needed for a fighting patrol. An officer led out a full platoon of twenty men, including me. Information had been received that a Ghurkha patrol had trouble clashing with a large number of Japs that had retreated back down the track again. The Ghurkhas had suffered some wounded and killed. It was thought the Japs would attempt a breakout so they decided to send a fighting patrol from our Company to check it out. We moved out in single file, no talking, passing through the village out in to the open countryside of the paddyfields which then quickly changed into six foot high reeds and marsh grass either side of the track. We were still alert and moved slowly, our weapons at the ready. Sections spread out either side of the track ready for action, but none came.

Later we heard shouting and crashing of many feet coming in our direction but we couldn't see anything behind the high screen of reeds and marsh grass. On the left hand side of the track our officer signalled to us to halt and we spaced out and took up positions of defence. The enemy seemed to be just yards away behind the reeds. We had our safety catches forward and were ready to fire. Then about ten yards in front of our officer, the leader of a large herd of cattle smashed down the tall reeds and high grass to cross the track, disappearing through the high grass. Behind were the rest of the herd with the drover still shouting at them in Burmese. They didn't notice us. We covered a further mile or so to open paddyfields. It was time to go back. We returned along the same track to base.

A day or two later we were detailed to do a standing patrol, just watching and listening. In our case to the dogs on the other side of the village. We were not sure if the dogs were just barking or whether there was a group of Japs in that part of the village. A village woman offered us some tea without milk or sugar in a saucer like bowl. We accepted thankfully and gave her some cigarettes. She liked that. It was a change from the thick type of cigar that most old Burmese women seemed to smoke. Later we did a little trading for fresh eggs for tins of our sardines.

After a few more patrols around the Pegu area we returned to Rangoon. There was talk of sending us in gliders to attack some coastal guns on the coast near Malaya but we were given a job in Rangoon for a couple of weeks, looking after Japanese prisoners of war at the local Jail. We felt like prisoners ourselves locked in that wild west style courtyard with a lot of Japs and iron bars all around. It wasn't easy guarding the prisoners. We were always on edge. We had been fighting these people and they were still our enemy. We were allowed to smoke and, as we did, the Jap prisoners, shuffled around and waited for us to throw away the nub-end of our cigarette. Then they would move forward and point to the cigarette end on the ground and hiss like a snake whilst standing to attention, bowing all the time until you gave him permission to take it up. I would let them pick them up and again they bowed and hissed until I waved them away. Some soldiers were not as soft as me and would simply put their foot on the cigarette and raise a rifle towards the prisoner and send them on their way with a volley of verbal abuse.

I had to escort a Jap officer to the cookhouse. He spoke good English and had a good sense of humour. However, when we reached the cookhouse his voice suddenly changed and he bellowed out orders, sounding like some sort of wild animal. It shocked me. He was tall and the smaller Japs ran round doing as he said. They brought him some rice cakes and he calmly and politely offered me one. They looked and smelt good, but I couldn't eat with him and refused. I didn't mind talking but I wasn't going to share his food. He was upset but as far as I was concerned he was the enemy and we were still at war. You don't eat with your enemies and that was that.

It was August 1945. We'd heard the Americans had dropped the atom bomb and were told the war would soon be over. We didn't count our chickens. We were used to that kind of talk and carried on as usual. Off duty we wandered around Rangoon and took in the sights. We were on our way back from the Chinese quarter after a meal when we heard a lot of noise and shooting. In all the commotion I thought the Japs had counter-attacked. Then we saw a jeep with some officers firing their pistols into the air. They were shouting and cheering saying that the Japs had surrendered. When we got back to the jail we told the Japs the news. They didn't believe us at first and shouted all sorts of abuse. Finally they realised it was true and became scared of what was to become of them. They needn't have worried, our treatment was far better than they gave our chaps. We knew that when we saw some of our chaps who had been Jap POWs at the docks waiting for the boat home. They were in a dreadful state and were really shocked and upset to hear how well we treated the enemy, but we couldn't take retribution. It wasn't our place to do so.

Around Christmas 1945, we were detailed to oversee the local dockworkers, or 'coolies' as we called them. They were loading and unloading the boats at the harbour and it was our job to see that everything went where it was supposed to and none went missing. We were allowed to keep any damaged fruit tins and often opened and helped ourselves to these perks. Unfortunately, I ate a dodgy tin of pears and caught tapeworm. I first noticed the end of it still wriggling in the remainder of the fruit I had just swallowed. I immediately threw the rest away. The MO was not that sympathetic and gave me a dressing down for not keeping the rest of the pear. He said that if I'd done so, he would have been able to identify the sex of the tapeworm, to see if it could breed inside me. I hadn't and so was hospitalised for nearly two weeks, to clear my system.

The war had ended but we didn't go home straight away. Things had to be sorted. We had to wait our turn. Anyway I'd signed up to 1949. I can't think of anything worse than to have survived that lot and be killed later on but that happened to some. Dick Pooley was killed. He stepped on a mine in Rangoon. He joined up in 1939 and had served in Africa and the Middle East as well as Burma, fighting the Germans and Italians as well as the Japs. What a way to go after all that. I wouldn't let that happen to me.

Soon after leaving hospital, I was detailed, with others, to track down bandits whilst some semblance of order and discipline returned to the country. Although the job was still difficult, the pressure was not as great. During rest periods some of the men would fish in the ponds that the locals had behind their huts. Some chaps even had Burmese girlfriends and they weren't pleased at all when it was time to move on, preferring to stay rather than go home. It was 1946 and my one month's home leave had come through. I returned to England on the 'Stamford Victory' sailing into Southampton. Some days after leaving Gibraltar, a cool breeze blew in our faces as we stood on the gun deck looking out to sea. We were in our thick battledress now, on our way home. Someone pointed to some dark clouds on the horizon, shouting, "There's England." We all laughed, saying how can that be England, it was just clouds. "You'll see." he said. He was right, some hours later Southampton was in plain view. As we approached, I had mixed feelings. Things were confusing and unreal after all that had happened, but as usual the army didn't give us time to think. The order came to parade and get ready to go ashore. Kit, kitbags and all other things had to be sorted out. As soon as we got ashore we boarded the train for home.

After my leave, I returned to duty at Maidstone Barracks but after a few days I felt sick during dinner and threw my food away. The NCO put me on a charge for wasting it. It didn't stick. Hours later I was in a military hospital with malaria. Ten days later I was a lot better and sent on to Kingston Convalescence Depot, but shortly after eating a bag of black cherries, I awakened a germ from my jungle days and found myself with amoebic dysentery, the worst type, and was immediately hospitalised. When I recovered I returned back to Kingston Camp for 'E' Board and was discharged.

It was 1947 when I travelled by train back to Birmingham and tried to make sense of what I'd been through. I didn't know what I was going to do in the future. Nobody gave us any advice. They left us to it. I thought of all the chaps that didn't make it back. There were wounded friends and I didn't know if they were alive. That was upsetting. I thought of Company Sergeant-Major Haines who was blinded at Kohima and continued to fight and encourage his men whilst been guided round the front line by a private. I thought of Jack Harman and others like him and his heroic actions when winning the Victoria Cross during the Siege. His actions no doubt saved us all. I remembered that a memorial had been erected there to commemorate those that had died. Its inscription reads:

> When you go home
> Tell them of us and say
> For your Tomorrow
> We gave our Today.

They say that the Battle of Kohima was the turning point of the Second World War in the Far East. I think I have done what the men who fought there would have wanted, told you about it. They mustn't be forgotten.

Robert Street

149

POSTSCRIPT

It was difficult after the war. Things weren't the same. I found it hard to re-adjust, but I was lucky, others couldn't. It was hell for them. Especially after what we'd all been through. You had to get on with it. There wasn't any counselling in those days. You were out of the army and they left you to it. I remember on one occasion hearing some fireworks going off and diving flat on to the ground instinctively, as if under fire. The girl I was with thought it was hilarious. I was embarrassed. She didn't understand really. Shortly after coming home I met a nice Irish girl who was lodging at my cousin's house; her name was Ann. Things seemed to be on the up and we married in July 1947.

I was registered disabled when I left the army, after all my illnesses and could only get low paid jobs. I was supposed to only do light work. The army gave me a pension though shillings a week. But I was married now and needed to earn more money. It was the end of 1947 when I got my first job. It was in an upholstery warehouse, sorting out all the different springs. The wages weren't much good, only five pounds a week. It was supposed to be easy work, but it wasn't. We had our first baby in 1948, a little girl, Linda. She became poorly. I remember being at work one day and heard Ann scream my name. It was so clear that I looked round, but she wasn't there. She was at home. Fifteen minutes later the boss called me in. He had received a phone call and sent me home. Linda had died of pneumonia. It was awful. Even after what I had done and seen, nothing could prepare me for that. It was a terrible feeling.

After a couple of years, I couldn't stick at the job ay longer, so my mother set me up in a second hand furniture shop. It had my name over the door, but it was her shop really. I did that until 1954 then worked for the BRS (British Road Services), checking the loads on and off lorries. That was boring. Fortunately, I got a transfer to loading the lorries. The money wasn't much better and the work was a lot harder, but I preferred that. We

150

had three more children by then. Another girl first, I was glad about that, especially for Ann, then two boys. I kept that job for nearly six years, but it didn't pay enough, not with a wife and three children to support. So in 1960 I passed my driving test and had another go at running a furniture shop. This time though it was to be my own. I sold new furniture, not second hand. I rented a shop in Camp Hill, near the city centre and gave it a go. Things went well at first and we soon moved out of my mother's house into our own. But it didn't last. The shop burnt down in the mid-sixties and I had to start again. It seemed that the luck I had during the war had worn thin. The shop was rebuilt and I started again. Just as I got back on my feet, my luck deserted me again. Ann died in 1970 and I was left with the three children to bring up. Later that year my daughter married. That was hard without Ann. The boys were still at school and I had to keep going for them. In 1979 I retired. The council wanted to widen the road. Mine was the last building standing. I wasn't going to start all over again; so I packed up. Then my luck changed for the better. The boys left school and were working, I met Val and we married in 1981.

When I look back I consider myself lucky. I've had a good life really. Yes, I've had hard times, but a lot of good times. I have seen the world; experienced and seen much more than some people could ever dream of. I have a lovely family with nine grandchildren and that's nice. I have more time now. When I was younger, I was too busy working so it's nice to play with the grandchildren now. They often come to see us. I still talk about the war, even to the grandchildren. They like that. I think it's important they know. Perhaps by telling them they can realise and not get involved should another war start. Don't get me wrong though, I wouldn't change it. Not the Arakan, Kohima, the Imphal Road, not a thing. I was proud to serve in the Royal West Kents and would do the same again. But it's different now. In these harvest years I want to enjoy my family and do my best for them. I also I think it's about leaving a little something behind for them to remember me. I think I've done that now.

161 Brigade Memorial

Tennis Court Memorial now